Network marketing professionals in praise of Keith Callahan's *Build to Last*

"Build to Last is absolute gold! Leadership is the foundation for success as a network marketer, and Keith does an incredible job breaking down the exact process to become a leader and create leaders within your own organization. Even though I'm a network marketing millionaire who's been involved in the industry for over ten years, I learned many things that I will start applying to my own business immediately. If you're looking to take your network marketing business to the next level, this is a MUST READ!"

— Josh Spencer, *multi-million-dollar earner*

"Imagine a book that gives you the step-by-step on creating a big business you can be proud of. This is it! Keith Callahan combines leadership development and network marketing so well, and provides tangible steps *anyone* can use to build a business. I have been in network marketing for six years. *Build to Last* gave me the tools I was missing as a leader. I feel more confident and ready to become the best leader I can be."

— Anita Miron, *million-dollar earner, achieved highest rank in her company*

"Keith Callahan really cares about people, and he sees the big picture. He understands that long-term success in network marketing comes down to two words: developing leaders. He's a master at breaking down the mindset, heartset, and skills you have to develop to do that. *Build to Last* is the blueprint. I'm grateful I met Keith early on, when I was struggling with my business. He shifted my mindset completely."

— Patrick Riehlman, *million-dollar earner*

"I've had the pleasure of working with Keith Callahan in my own business for six years, and it wasn't until I read *Build to Last* that I finally got inside his brain fully! On top of feeling completely on fire for my business and having a reignited belief in my own capabilities, I have been implementing Keith's one-on-one mentoring pointers with top distributors in my downline. I'm seeing them mentor their own downline, gain confidence, and grow their businesses with simple, duplicatable steps. I will definitely gift this book to anyone new I bring on!"

— Candice Talbot, *million-dollar earner*

"*Build to Last* gives you not only a step-by-step guide to attracting leaders, but the skillset to help identify them, work with them, and build trust with them. Very few network marketing books delve into how to mentor leaders within your downline to create the business of your dreams. Bravo, Keith, for taking on the missing puzzle piece for so many distributors, and making it accessible so they, too, can build to last!"

— Leslie Kortes, *multi-million-dollar earner, achieved highest rank in her company*

"*Build to Last* is the go-to book for mastering sustainable success in network marketing. If you've been looking for the 'secret sauce' in our industry, you've found it! Keith Callahan lays out before you – in a systematic, duplicatable, and easy-to-follow manner – the foundation to achieve long-lasting financial success. And freedom of time as well…Keith is an authentic leader of leaders with a generous heart who has paved the way for thousands. I will undoubtedly gift this book to my entire team and all future newcomers."

— Lisa Hansen, *million-dollar earner*

"You know a great book when you want to highlight every sentence. *Build to Last* is the most practical, applicable, and encouraging book I've read on multilevel marketing in my eight-year career. It's forthright, sincere, and speaks to both the beginner and the veteran in our industry. This book will be an on-boarding must-read for my team."

— Lindsay Stay, *7-figure annual earner,*
achieved highest rank in her company

"Build to Last is a deep dive into the heart and mind of a successful leader in network marketing. Keith Callahan shares his wisdom in small bites that can be implemented with ease and used to build your leadership confidence instantly. This profession can inspire people like no other, and with the tips and insight that Keith offers in his book, you can truly thrive in a business you love."

— Milan Jensen, *million-dollar earner, speaker at*
"Most Powerful Women in Network Marketing" conference

"One of the best books I've read on creating a legacy – step by step – with your network marketing business. Each chapter is rich in content that every marketing professional should know as well as specific action steps that tie knowledge to action. As someone in network marketing for eight years, I appreciate content directed to a seasoned distributor who wants to continue to grow and reach new heights. Simultaneously *Build to Last* will help brand new distributors launch their business…
Since I've applied Keith Callahan's concepts and systems for leading as a professional hands-on mentor, I've seen more success and growth in my organization. Read this book!"

— Dara Distel, *million-dollar earner,*
achieved highest rank in her company

"The lack of long-term systems in my first and only network marketing business – with massive early success – has cost me years of frustration and loss of potential income. Practical systems are critical in short- and long-term planning for the longevity of your business. Keith Callahan's book gives you methods, applications, and tools for a system to grow and nourish your team, and create a thick, healthy downline. I highly recommend *Build to Last* for network marketers at all levels."

— Doug "Coach" Couch,
multi-million-dollar earner, celebrity spokesperson

"*Build to Last* offers straightforward and detailed steps that network marketing business owners can take, starting where they currently are, to build long-term sustainable income. I have not found a book out there like this one and will share *Build to Last* with every one of my leaders."

— Jessica Vandeberghe, *million-dollar earner*

"I kept getting goose bumps reading *Build to Last* because I felt like Keith Callahan was writing for *me*! Although I'm a multi-million-dollar earner and the distributor who has achieved 'Top 10' the most often in my company, I realized I have become a leader of followers, not of leaders! My business's success depends completely on my efforts and not the efforts of my team. What an aha moment for me! I plan to re-read *Build to Last* and start implementing Keith's well crafted system for developing leaders. I'm excited to get the book in the hands of my team. Thank you, Keith, for sharing your steps to success. It's definitely going to help this leader develop more leaders!"

— Melissa McAllister, *multi-million-dollar earner*

"*Build to Last* equates to true freedom. This book will teach you how to build a rock-solid network marketing foundation using methods that will leave you feeling deeply fulfilled and proud of your legacy...During seven years in this industry, I have tried every different way to build. I wish someone had given me this book the day I decided to build my network marketing business."

— Andrea Crowder, *multi-million-dollar earner*

"Keith Callahan has created a fantastic resource in this book that shares the 'untold system' of building a network marketing business through leadership. In my experience, leaders are what generate longevity, stability, and financial freedom in our industry. *Build to Last* is the blueprint for how to find those people and develop them into your highest earners and beyond. But as Keith reveals, the real gift is the person you become in order to have a life-changing impact on others."

— Kristina Sullins, *multi-million-dollar earner, team of 25,000+, achieved highest rank in her company*

"*Build to Last* is great for people who are serious about network marketing. I had the privilege of learning from Keith Callahan firsthand during my first six months in this business. I followed all the steps he told me to, no questions asked, and earned $1 million in my first five years. I was a wife and mom of two girls, a two-month-old and a four-year-old, when I began building this business. I didn't *have* the time, I made the time to build a legacy for my family."

— Nicole L Jones, *million-dollar earner*

"Keith Callahan has written a must-read guide for anyone desiring long-term success in network marketing. Read this book and you will learn how to grow from where you are right now into who you need to become to create a true legacy."

— Karri LeGault, *former middle-school math teacher, 6-figure earner within first two years*

"Our past does not have to be our compass for the future. This truth is the compelling drive that has built Keith Callahan a multi-million-dollar business and the legacy of hundreds of leaders' lives changed forever. Keith is a man of highest integrity and character, and one of the finest leaders I have worked with during my 40 years of mentoring and training multilevel marketing professionals all over the world. His book articulates the simple truths of building generational leaders, and gives you a game plan and structure to build a legacy business."

— Craig Holiday, *8-figure earner, international mentor*

Build to Last

Build to Last

A Step-by-step Guide to Long-term Network Marketing Success

KEITH CALLAHAN

Published by Ten Hands Publishing
PO Box 172
Sherborn, Massachusetts 01770

ISBN: 978-0-578-21240-1

This book is dedicated to you,
the next leader in network marketing.
I believe in you and know you have what it takes.
Now make it happen.

CONTENTS

INTRODUCTION

Have you ever wondered why a select few experience success in network marketing at the highest levels, year after year, while everyone else struggles?

Is it because they're simply better than you and more deserving? Success at the highest levels is for others, but not for you? Is it because they work harder than you? Is it because they got in at the top of the pyramid? Maybe they have a better sponsor or are on a better team?

The answer: none of the above.

The real reason a select few experience success at the highest levels, while the majority struggle, is simply their MINDSET. *The super successful build with the mindset of a CEO while everyone else builds with the mindset of an employee.* You can put in all the effort you want and work ten times harder than everyone else, but if your mindset is that of an employee, you will get the results of an employee, at best. On the other hand, if you have the mindset of a CEO and take the daily actions of a CEO, you're setting yourself up to get the results of a CEO.

Here's the good news: You have the ability to change your mindset and attract success at the highest levels.

A Guide for Achieving Success

Build to Last lays out the intentional way successful network marketing professionals build – the way a CEO builds a business. The cornerstone of a build-to-last business is leadership and relationships. It's built by first becoming a leader yourself and then developing those you mentor into leaders. The end goal is a business that thrives for years to come and does so – here's the important part – with or without you. In my opinion this is the only logical way to build a network marketing team because it allows you to do two things: help the most people and earn the highest, long-term, stable income.

Personal Leadership and Leading Others

Build to Last has two sections. Section One, "Personal Leadership," focuses on the personal transformation and the personal development necessary to lead others. It explores the mindset, philosophy, and approach that characterize people who achieve the highest levels of success in network marketing. This section is more about who you must *become* than what you have to *do*. Section Two, "Leading Others," is the "what you have to do" section of the book. It's the nuts and bolts of how to attract, identify, and eventually mentor leaders. You will learn how to position yourself as a leader in the minds of others and the steps necessary to take people all the way from prospect to being a leader of their own team.

Who This Book Is For

The information, principles, and actions in this book are not for everyone in network marketing.

I wrote this book with a few assumptions in mind:

First, you are already in the industry and have a basic understanding of our profession and terminology used within the industry. This is not an introduction to network marketing.

Second, you recognize the potential in our industry, but you haven't personally experienced that high-level, long-lasting success – yet.

Third, you are coachable and willing to put in the work to achieve the highest levels of success in our industry, but you need a guide showing you how.

Will This Work For You?

Right now, you might be thinking, "Does this work? Is this going to work for me? Can I do this?" The answer is YES. This will absolutely work for you, and you can do it.

Those are not the right questions to ask though. The question is not "Will this work?" The real question to ask yourself is "Am I willing to do what it takes?" The important word there is *willing*. Are you willing to do the necessary work to become the person you need to become?

Reading this book and absorbing the information is not enough. *Build to Last* is not a pleasure read. It's a resource showing you how to become a leader. Don't just sit on what you read. Knowledge without implementation is useless. Read this book, learn the principles, then go out there and take action!

FREE Bonus Materials

Throughout this book I refer to many systems, checklists, and workflows I use in my business. I've put together FREE bonus materials, including PDFs, webpage links, and audios, for your benefit. You can find these bonus materials at KeithCallahan.com/book. They are all on one page, and you can download them all at one time.

WHO IS KEITH CALLAHAN?

If you're looking for an author with all the credentials, degrees, and esteemed letters after his name, then you have come to the wrong place. On the other hand, if you're looking for someone who has been there and done that, learned on the streets, came from nothing, and built his way to financial freedom as a network marketing professional, well then, I'm that guy.

I was cautioned not to be so transparent, but I'm choosing to share my full story anyway. For you to embrace and take action on the principles I teach in *Build to Last*, you need to trust me. The best way for me to earn your trust is through honesty and vulnerability.

So here is my story…

The Dream
My dream growing up was to be rich. It wasn't about financial freedom or the ability to do what I want. I just wanted to be rich. I loved the lure of the big house, the fancy cars…all of it. In my young, immature, egocentric, male mind, I mistakenly thought life was all about money.

Around the time I finished college (I say "finished" instead of "graduated" because I never did), this country came into one of the biggest real estate booms ever seen. I recognized the opportunity and began looking to buy my first property. It came fast, and I bought and sold a house in the same day for a profit of $33,000. How's that for a day's work?

Over the next five years, a partner and I set up a business flipping homes. We began one house at a time. Soon we saw deals we wanted to make but didn't have the money to complete, and we started offering partnerships to friends and family. The partners put up money for repairs and holding costs in exchange for 25 percent of the profits. The financial influx – along with hiring good contractors – allowed us to go from flipping a single home at a time to 10 homes at a time. We were making more money doing less work, and our friends and family were enjoying returns of 25 to 50 percent on their money in three to six months! We bought and sold over 50 homes, and everything was moving along as smooth as could be.

Bankrupting the Dream

So many of my early mentors warned me: "Make sure you don't rush things." "Don't bite off more than you can chew." "Don't over-leverage yourself." "Make sure you get out early, don't be caught when the market turns." But the cocky 20-something-year-old thought he knew more than these seasoned pros did...and got burned BIG TIME.

The market turned. My partner and I found prices dropping and homes not selling. All of the sudden, we owned 11 single-family homes, all with mortgages, all with friends and family who had invested in them, all upside down (we owed more than a house was worth) and unsellable! Life got ugly on a personal level for me. I had to file bankruptcy for the business and personal bankruptcy – the hardest, most demoralizing, scary, and defeating business experience I have known. I remember my bankruptcy attorney calling me "fortunate" to go through it all at such a young age. He told me I was a bright guy and would emerge so much stronger. At the time I could hardly see bankruptcy as a positive, but he was right. The experience dropped me to my knees as a cocky, young boy, and I stood up as a humbled, compassionate, disciplined man.

A shining light in the whole ordeal was keeping my word to everyone who invested with us. My parents brought me up to be a man of my word and have integrity. I used any and all profits from previous deals to pay back our friends and family. Some got their money right away and some received payments over time, but everyone got their money back. This was a major character-building experience for me.

Rebuilding the Dream

My process of rebuilding was not just about business. I had to build a new person – physically, spiritually, emotionally, and financially. All of this came about in a way I least expected.

Two friends and I committed to a 90-day physical transformation program. (We didn't know then that the producer was a network marketing company.) Prior to this, I had the habit of jumping from one undertaking to another without finishing anything. This time, I completed the 90 days and got the physical transformation, but what happened on the *inside* far surpassed the physical. Sticking with the entire program was a huge, personal accomplishment. I wanted to quit many times, but I didn't. After the completion of those first 90 days, I turned a weakness into a strength: I'm now really careful about what I commit to; and when I do commit, I can be trusted to finish.

For the next two years, I continued to be a customer

of this network marketing company. I was in the best shape of my life, I was happy, I had married the woman of my dreams, and we had just had our first daughter. Amy was on maternity leave, and we were trying to figure out our next steps. We really wanted Amy to be home to raise our children. At the time, I was working 12-hour days, leaving the house at 5:30 in the morning and coming home between 8 and 9 at night. Although I was making good money and Amy was able to stay home, this came at huge personal expense. I didn't have the time I craved with my daughter, and I had no energy left for my wife when I got home.

And then it happened…

One of the annual ceremonies of the spiritual path I follow is called "Vision Quest." It's a four-day ceremony of personal prayer to ask the Creator for help and guidance and a "vision" for your life. This particular year, my prayer centered around my professional life. I needed a change, but I had no idea what that change would look like. On the fourth day, I got the answer: "Become a network marketing professional with the company that changed your life." This scared the hell out of me. I had no idea how the business worked or how I could make a living. All I knew was I loved the products and programs of the company because of that original 90-day fitness challenge.

Realizing the Dream

When I first became a network marketing professional, my mentor told me I needed to find a WHY that motivated me. My WHY was clear and direct.

I want to be able to do WHAT I WANT in life.

I want to be able to do it with WHO I WANT.

I want to be able to do it WHEN I WANT.

I want to spend time with my family and friends. Hold each of my children daily, play with them, change their diapers, send them to the best schools. Drive the cars, live in the house, move to the town I want. Go snowboarding, hiking, mountain biking, eat out when I want.

I still had a full-time job when I began dedicating about 10 hours a week to my network marketing business. I squeezed every last minute out of those 10 hours. I was on a mission, determined to become a full-time network marketing professional. I did that within one year, and my life will never be the same.

I remember crying while writing on Facebook, "I am now a full-time network marketing professional." I was free, and I was rich. What made me rich wasn't the money – the crazy money (what I call "monopoly money") still hadn't come. I was rich because I truly had the ability to do what I wanted, when I wanted, with who I wanted.

Living the Dream

For the last nine years I've been able to work from home. I make my own schedule. I spend time with my kids during the days. I drop them off and pick them up from school. I cook dinner and play with them. I have watched them grow day by day, and haven't missed a thing.

In the process Amy and I have been able to pay off all of our debt (except our mortgage). We moved to the town of our dreams and bought the house of our dreams. We drive the cars we want and send our kids to an excellent school.

Reluctantly, I want to share my first eight years' earnings as a network marketing professional. It's uncomfortable and feels egotistical to include personal financial information for the world to see, but I feel it's important. If I'm going to teach you how my leaders and I have built our business and to recommend you build the same way, you need to know the results that my approach is capable of producing: long-term, high-level, sustainable income.

Annual earnings:
Year 1 $12,847 (started business in May)
Year 2 $91,559
Year 3 $260,899
Year 4 $479,925
Year 5 $686,623
Year 6 $762,896
Year 7 $829,696
Year 8 $857,295

Income disclaimer: As in any independent business, the level of success or achievement is dependent upon the commitment, skill level, drive, and desire to succeed of the individual. Success results only from effective sales efforts, which require hard work, diligence, and leadership.

Paying the Dream Forward

I went from an extremely low point to living a dream life. And that blessing doesn't go unnoticed by me. After my personal goals were met, I turned my attention to helping others do the same. I didn't think my business could be more rewarding, but it just keeps getting better. There's nothing like the feeling you get by helping people completely change their lives.

My new WHY, what really drives me now, is teaching others how to build their network marketing businesses to last. Month after month, I get to be on the receiving end of someone thanking me for changing her or his life. All that I'm doing, though, is passing on information from the many mentors and teachers in my life.

I wrote *Build to Last* to pass on to you an approach I put to work in my business and personal life. A way of building your network marketing business so it helps you create a life doing what you want, when you want, with who you want.

I hope you enjoy this book and use it as a guide to building the life of your dreams.

Much love,
Keith Callahan

Section One

PERSONAL LEADERSHIP

"Personal Leadership" is more about
who you must become than
what you have to do.

After reading this section, you will no longer see yourself as simply a distributor for your company. You will see yourself as the CEO of a big business. You will understand the importance of leadership and relationships in building your business so it lasts. You will see the enormity of the opportunity you are sitting on and the generational impact you can have. You will learn the seven core philosophies of leaders in the network marketing industry and how to apply them to your business. You will learn how to create a personal development plan specific to building to last. You will learn how to identify areas you need to improve upon and how to measure your "personal development success" in those areas. You will learn the importance of having one overarching, long-term goal and how to select that goal. Finally, you will learn how to direct your focus so you start attracting the success available as a network marketing professional.

Chapter 1

BUILD TO LAST AND LEADERSHIP

*The function of leadership is to produce
more leaders, not more followers.*
— Ralph Nader

Three years into building my network marketing business, I went on a spiritual retreat with my family. During the two weeks we were away and unplugged from all technology, my team added over 800 new distributors. Upon returning, I found no voicemails, no text messages, and no social media messages awaiting me. Not a single person contacted or needed me. Our team was growing like crazy, and it was growing without me! The reason for this is simple. I had developed leaders on my team.

Almost a decade into network marketing, the opportunity has been financially rewarding, but more importantly it has given me and my leaders *freedom*. Freedom to create life on our terms – to spend our time doing what we want, when we want, with who we want. We have intentionally built our businesses to serve the lifestyle we want to live.

Our way of building is a synthesis of my mentors' teachings, and my own trial and error over the last decade. I was fortunate to encounter mentor-leader Craig Holiday right from the start. Craig mentored me to become a leader of myself, my family, and my team. When I modeled what he taught me and mentored others in my organization, we began to have tremendous success, and that mentorship duplicated. Those I mentored started mentoring their distributors the way we were taught, and so on.

Because of the leadership and success we had on our team, leaders of other teams within our company began asking me to speak to their leaders. Corporate leadership caught on and invited me to share what we were doing with other leaders in our company. Eventually leaders from other companies asked me to speak on their calls and teach their leaders what we were doing.

After each training, I would get messages from leaders saying the same thing: "I WISH I HAD THIS TRAINING WHEN I FIRST STARTED."

I realized what I had to offer was valuable. It is a missing piece in our industry that so many "would-be leaders" just like you need. A simple philosophy, with basic principles to follow, teaching you how to grow a business that's built to last.

I've been able to watch leader after leader go on to have the success they always dreamed of after integrating the principles in *Build to Last*, and I'm excited to share them with you.

Leadership and Relationships

Leadership and relationships are the cornerstone of a network marketing business that lasts. Without leadership and deep relationships, you might have some short-term success, but attrition will begin showing up in your business, and it will eventually fall apart from the bottom up.

Our industry has two distinct types of leader: leaders of followers and leaders of leaders. Leadership expert John Maxwell offers the best description of each. A leader of followers needs to be needed, he says, and a leader of leaders wants to be exceeded. This principle is so important I want to repeat it for you:

> *Leaders of followers need to be needed,*
> *and leaders of leaders want to be exceeded.*

Leader of Followers Versus Leader of Leaders

Leaders of followers have the ability to lead followers but not other leaders.

They are usually charismatic people with big personalities. Leaders of followers always want the spotlight. They want to be up on stage, getting recognized at the annual company convention. Leaders of followers lead people who are dependent on them. They get constant texts, emails, and direct messages because everyone on their team depends on them for answers to all questions on a daily basis. Their team looks to them for leadership because they're all followers. When leaders of followers go on vacation, their business takes a big hit.

In contrast, the main goal of leaders of leaders isn't necessarily to achieve the highest ranks themselves, it is to empower the others on their team to hit the highest ranks. They want to be sitting in the audience at the company convention watching the leaders they've developed walk across stage, getting recognized. When I developed my organization, I focused on building a team of such leaders who would grow their own teams.

Word of Caution

Not everyone you mentor will become a leader, and not every leader you mentor will become a leader of leaders. To put this in perspective, consider the breakdown on my team today, as I'm writing: I have about 30,000 distributors; of those, about 100 are leaders. But only two or three can be considered leaders of leaders. That's how rare a leader of leaders is.

The purpose of this book is to help YOU (not everyone on your team) become a leader of leaders. This path involves creating other leaders, not necessarily leaders of leaders. It will be rare for you to develop one.

How the Numbers Play Out

I love talking with people in our industry, bouncing ideas off each other and learning from each other. During a conversation with my friend – let's call him Bill – who is also a professional network marketer, we got into the ins and outs of how our businesses are structured, how our income is derived, and more. At the time I brought in a slightly higher income than he did. We both had been working for the same amount of time with our respective companies, which have similar comp plans. From an outsider's perspective, everything was pretty much equal. The main difference between our businesses was that Bill operated as a leader and I operate as a leader of leaders.

Leader versus *leader of leaders*. There's a small difference in words but a world of difference in results.

Bill is a great recruiter. He consistently brings in 50-plus distributors a month. Month after month, all year long. That's his main focus. I'm currently the opposite of Bill when it comes to recruiting. Five is the most distributors I've ever recruited in one month. Needless to say, given that I bring in a max of five distributors a month and Bill brings in 50, our businesses looked very different from the start.

Here is the piece you might not expect: as I'm writing *Build to Last*, I have a team of over 30,000 distributors, and Bill has about 3,000 distributors. How can that be? Why am I sponsoring one-tenth of the distributors but have a team that is ten times the size of Bill's? That is the power of becoming a leader of leaders. The power of duplicating leadership in your downline. Our industry is one of duplication and developing leaders, NOT of being a great one-man show. Bill knows that if he takes any time off, his business will implode. His business is built and predicated upon him showing up every single day and doing the work.

If I step away from my business, not only is it going to survive, it's going to thrive. Thrive, because we've built our business with a solid foundation, and we've built it through duplicating leadership. I'm not just the leader of "my team," but I've also created other leaders who are growing their own teams. Those leaders will continue to grow their teams with or without me because they are no longer dependent on me.

Change Your Focus, Change Your Results

Bill and I both dedicate the same amount of time to our businesses, but we focus on different areas. His main focus is recruiting as many people as he can and putting them into his training systems. My focus is recruiting a smaller number, spending time with them, and working to develop them into leaders. In the beginning, Bill's approach allows you to help more people and earn more money, more quickly. However, over time, through developing leaders and the law of exponential growth, my business model creates an organization that surpasses Bill's.

Building a team of leaders, rather than followers, allows you to create the freedom in your life to do what you want, when you want, with who you want. Becoming a leader of leaders gives you freedom in your business and it gives you freedom in your life.

As for Bill, he began following the model I teach in this book and is well on his way to becoming a leader of leaders. With his recruiting skills and the addition of becoming a leader of leaders, Bill is in a position to far surpass what I've built.

Little Nicole Jones Versus 14 Yoga Studios

Following is a story about two distributors who signed with me when I first started in network marketing. One of them – let's call him Michael – owned 14 yoga studios with over 150 instructors. The company I'm a distributor for is in the health and wellness realm, so it was a perfect fit for this clientele. Michael introduced me to all 150 of his instructors. "I just signed up as a distributor," he said to them. "This is something I think you should check out. Keith Callahan is going to be contacting you in the next couple of days." In addition, Michael allowed me to put up flyers in all 14 studios, with my contact information for our nutritional products.

At the same time, I signed on Nicole Jones, a woman I went to high school with. Nicole was married, had just had her second child, and didn't want to go back to work. When she told me she wanted to get healthy and fit herself, I told her about the opportunity to be a distributor with our company. Nicole started using our products and working on her own health and wellness. She then shared her results with friends and family, who also started using our products and working on their health and wellness.

Looking at the opportunities with both Nicole and Michael, most people think (as did I) the huge opportunity is with Michael and the yoga studios.

Here's what happened.

In month 1, the yoga studio came out strong. We sold $3,000 in products that month. Nicole came out excited but didn't produce nearly as much. She sold about $400 in products to her friends and family that month.

Month 2 rolls around and the yoga studio sold $3,000-$4,000 in products. Nicole continued to do what she was doing. She had reoccurring orders from people she had helped the previous month and some new people coming in, for a total of $800 in orders that month. She also signed a few working distributors. This is where the shift began.

In month 6, the yoga studios continued bringing in approximately the same $4,000 in retail sales. By then, I had talked with all the yoga instructors at the studios. Some signed up and did a little, some signed up and didn't do much, and some never signed up at all. Meanwhile Nicole had been chugging along with her own retail sales and building a team. In month 6, Nicole's team generated over $15,000 in sales.

At month 12, Nicole's team generated almost seven times the volume and income of the yoga studios. They were at about $3,000 a month, and Nicole was over $20,000 a month.

Fast forward three years. The yoga studios were generating about $1,500 a month in products. Nicole's team was generating over $150,000 a month! That's 100 times the volume. Nicole is a leader. She had built a team. She had duplication. She was developing other leaders in her downline. She was making over $5,000 a week – and growing!

Income disclaimer: As in any independent business, the level of success or achievement is dependent upon the commitment, skill level, drive, and desire to succeed of the individual. Success results only from effective sales efforts, which require hard work, diligence, and leadership.

Leaders, Leaders, Leaders

When you are looking to build to last, set your mind on recruiting and developing leaders. Your goal is NOT just to become a leader yourself (although you need to do that first). Your ultimate goal is to become a leader of leaders within your company. What you need to be thinking in the morning when you get up, all throughout the day, and until you go to bed at night is: *I'm looking for leaders.* Personally, I would rather have one true leader than 100 people who are half in. That's how valuable a leader is to you if you want to become a leader of leaders.

Want to know if you have this leadership piece down? Ask yourself how your team is doing. Not how are *you* doing, how is your *team* doing? How would they do without you? Without duplicating leadership, you haven't built to last. You have a business that is dependent on YOU.

Action Steps

1. Make a list of the "leaders of leaders" you admire in your company or within the network marketing industry as a whole.

2. Working with the above list, what do they do differently than others? What type of people are they? How do they make other people feel? What skills do they possess that you admire?

3. To assist yourself in training your mind to think leadership thoughts and "becoming a leader of leaders" thoughts, put reminders around your house, in your car, on your phone, and elsewhere, saying things like:
- I am becoming a leader of leaders.
- I'm looking for leaders, not followers.
- I am a leader.

Chapter 2

BUILD TO LAST AND LEGACY

*Leadership is not about the next election,
it's about the next generation.*
— Simon Sinek

Network marketing trainers, companies, and leadership all love talking about "finding your WHY." And not just any old WHY, but "a WHY that makes you cry." These WHYs come in different forms depending on a distributor's current life situation. Common WHYs include to stay at home with your kids, to pay off your credit cards, to go on a vacation, to get out of debt, to experience greater meaning in life.

When we talk about finding your WHY, initially it's your reason for getting started in the network marketing business – something that excites and motivates you, and holds you accountable when you're less motivated to do the daily work. As you progress in the business, your WHY progresses with you. As you start to accomplish your goals and see success, your personal situation changes. Maybe that credit card is paid off or you are now able to stay at home or take the vacation.

The Ultimate WHY – Leaving a Legacy

I want to share with you what I believe to be the ultimate WHY for a professional network marketer. Leaving a legacy. If you're a true leader of leaders (or that's what you're striving for), leaving a legacy eventually becomes your WHY. Leaders of leaders' WHY becomes bigger than themselves.

Leaving a legacy is about making life better for those who follow you than it was for you. It's about showing people how to live better than they ever dreamed possible. Leaving a legacy starts with you, touches those you directly influence, and eventually leads to generational change.

Leaving a legacy has nothing to do with money. That is an inheritance. An inheritance leaves money in someone's checking account. Your legacy leaves something in their heart and in their soul. Leaving a legacy is about you becoming the best possible version of yourself, and being that person day in and day out. By becoming your best self, you become the type of person who can effect positive change on those you touch – people you work with directly in your downline, family members, people in your community. Your living and teaching a certain way of life influences them. It's the feeling you give people. The confidence you instill in them. Leaving a legacy is about you being the person who tells them they're good enough, they're worthy, and they can live the big, beautiful, bold dream they have tucked away. Leaving a legacy is about living up to your full potential, and then mentoring others through modeling to live up to their full potential.

The effect of the work you have done doesn't stop there. For over ten years now both in my personal life and in my business, I have followed the principle of "seven generations of change," which I learned from a Native American elder. In short, the principle says:

Our lives are impacted by the seven generations before us, and our lives will impact the next seven generations.

Our focus is on the latter. If I become my best self as a husband, father, mentor, leader, community member, and friend, this obviously has a positive effect on the type of life I live. It affects my happiness, my overall sense of wellbeing, my contentment, my sense of purpose, my relationships. When I work to become my best self, I get the positive life experiences and emotions that go along with that. It also touches my children because of what I model for them. They learn and model this behavior. And my children model for my grandchildren, who model for my great grandchildren, and so on. This is the concept of seven generations of change, which helped me realize my life is so much bigger than just me.

Considering seven generations also made things simpler for me, and it can make things simpler for you too. When we look at our decisions and the effects they will have seven generations down the road, the "right" decision becomes clear. When we look at the hard things we need to do and realize that it's not just going to affect us or our kids but the next seven generations, the hard things seem that much more worthwhile. It becomes natural to think more deeply and act more wisely about our choices and actions. We think more about what we say, how we spend our time, even what our thoughts are.

What Are You Leaving in the Hearts and Souls of Others?

I'm not talking about learning new skills or tactics. Think about people who changed the course of history for their generation and the generations after them – leaders like Nelson Mandela, Mother Teresa, Martin Luther King, Jr., Mahatma Gandhi, Oprah, Rosa Parks. When you think about them and the change they initiated, you think of their way of being in the world. The firmness in their mission and vision. Their unshakeable faith. These leaders stood for what they believed in and their vision and dream created movements, which led to generational change. We who followed after Mandela, Gandhi, Mother Teresa, and Martin Luther King, Jr., for generations to come live differently because of them.

What are you leaving in the hearts and souls of those you touch? Is it something you want passed down for seven generations? Who are you modeling? You don't have to be a Gandhi or Rosa Parks (although you could be), but you can model your behaviors on the way they lived. You can bring that type of energy into your everyday life and your business.

Don't make the mistake of dreaming small with your business. So many people get involved in network marketing and don't understand the enormity of the opportunity.

Set the Intention for What You're Building

A few years back, a handful of the male leaders in our company (which is 90 percent female) decided to create a company-wide event for men. We wanted to train other men on what we, as male leaders, were doing to see success.

We brought in high-profile speakers from outside our company and leaders within our company. My personal sponsor Bob and I were asked to do a presentation together. We chose to address the topic of leaving a legacy. I was excited about the opportunity to speak, and even more eager to listen to the other presenters at this event. I had looked up to these men for years. Many were founding distributors with our company, putting them a "generation" ahead of me. I had studied many of them from afar and never gotten close with them. I just kept my head down and did my thing for the most part.

During the event, I had a huge internal shift. I had flown below the radar in our company and was never comfortable in the spotlight. I had had a mental construct of seeing the other male leaders within our company as "more" or "better" than I was, even if I earned more than they did and had a larger organization. My big internal shift came because of the feedback Bob and I received around our presentation. At the end of the event, men we admired shared with us that our presentation was completely "eye opening." They had never before come across the leaving-a-legacy principle or our approach to building our business. We heard over and over that people intended to implement everything we taught. The biggest aha for me came from seasoned distributors saying they wished they'd had this training from the start.

I began to realize that not only did Bob and I build differently than others in our industry, but our intention from the outset was different, and that intention led to significantly different results over time.

Income Is Not the Real Gift, a Changed Life Is

Many of us make the mistake of thinking income is the big gift and promise of our industry. The income you can make (if you do it right) will indeed far surpass your expectations. That's not the real gift in this business, though. The real gift is being the person you have to become in order to earn the income. That's the gift. There are no shortcuts to the top in this industry. You have to become a person capable of achieving success yourself before you can mentor others to success. The blessing of this business is that the more bright, shiny, happy, content, loving, and gracious you become, the more success you see. The better version of you that you become, the more you earn. The money is the byproduct of a better you!

Becoming the best possible version of yourself, so you can help others become the best possible version of themselves, is not easy work. It's simple – and in the remaining three chapters of this section, I'm going to show you how to do it – but it's not easy. The reward is a changed life, for you, the people you touch, and the seven generations down the road.

Action Steps

It's time to dream big and dream beautiful. Set aside a few hours to create in your mind the life you want to live and the impact you want to leave. Work through the following exercises in a quiet place where you won't be interrupted.

1. Think 5 years into the future. Who have you become? What is your ideal self? What will your day-to-day activities look like? What will your relationships be like? What type of home or homes will you have? Will you be traveling? Think of all aspects of your life and describe the most beautiful vision you can.

2. Think 20 years into the future. Who have you become? What is your ideal self? What will your day-to-day activities look like? What will your relationships be like? What type of home or homes will you have? Will you be traveling? Think of all aspects of your life and describe the most beautiful vision you can.

3. Think about the generations who are going to follow you. What type of impact would you like to have on them? What do you want to leave in their hearts? What is YOUR LEGACY going to be? Write it out.

Chapter 3

THE BUILD-TO-LAST MINDSET

Leadership is practiced not so much in words as in attitude and in actions.
— Harold S. Geneen

A leader's philosophy on life and how to build a network marketing business is significantly different from that of distributors who are not leaders. In order to start leading others, you must first lead yourself. Following are seven core philosophies for leading yourself.

1. Leaders focus on who they are becoming more than what they are getting.

A leader's mindset is not about activities, rewards, or accolades. It's about who she or he is becoming. A leader knows it's not possible to hold the title or rank of leader long-term without *becoming* a person capable of doing so. Leading is about changing yourself from the inside out. Leaders are focused on who they are becoming versus what they're getting.

2. Leaders don't just believe they can, they know they will.

There is a vital difference between believing you can do something and knowing without a doubt that you will do it. Those who become leaders in network marketing don't just believe they can achieve success, they know they will.

Here is a quick story to illustrate my point.

My personal sponsor, Bob, tried to get me to become a distributor for six months. He messaged me over and over. I got sick of getting his messages, tired of hearing about this "opportunity," fed up with all the pictures on social media. I didn't want to hear it anymore. I was annoyed enough to "un-friend" Bob on Facebook. I told him I didn't want to do this "network marketing thing" that he was involved in.

Not only did I not want to do it, I thought Bob had gone crazy. During this time he was working full-time, married with two children and two other children from a previous marriage. He kept telling me he intended to shut down his law practice and be a full-time network marketing professional. My reaction: "Dude, you're crazy. I would love to do something like that. It sounds great, but this is the real world. You're married. You've got four kids. You've got a law practice. You've got your home. You have all these responsibilities. You can't just shut down your legal office and go full-time into network marketing." But Bob had a vision of making that a reality in his life.

So what happened? Why did everything change for me? Why did I decide, one day, to sign up and build a large organization? Because Bob had an internal shift at our company's annual event.

Prior to that event, Bob believed in our products. He believed in the business opportunity. He believed in the leaders at the corporate level and the leaders within the network. He also believed he could be successful at this business. He had already had some success. Then the shift happened. At the annual event Bob met others who were having big success. He met some of the leaders at corporate. And he met some of the leaders in the field. Something clicked for Bob in the process of meeting all those leaders. He went from believing he could do this to *knowing without a doubt* that he was going to do it.

That piece is so important I want to highlight it. Bob shifted from *believing* he could do it to *knowing* he was going to do it. As a result, his energy changed. His mindset changed. And everything in his business changed. After he moved from just believing he could to knowing he would, I decided to sign up, as did many other people he had been messaging. That's when Bob laid the foundation of his business and went on to become a full-time network marketing professional.

This *knowing* piece is the internal shift many would-be leaders never make. Where are you right now? Do you know without a doubt you're going to build a large organization? You can go through the motions of talking with people all you want, but until you make the shift, they won't be attracted to you or want to join you. Once you make the shift, they'll see and feel that you are going to run with this opportunity and make something of it, with or without them. I saw that in Bob. I recognized that he saw something, and I didn't want to be left behind.

3. Leaders don't just "show up," they show up with their mind right.

When I signed up to become a distributor, I wanted to build a big business and I knew it was possible. In order to do that, though, I needed to get to that place of knowing it was actually going to happen *for me.*

I needed to change my mindset from "can't" to "can," from "impossible" to "possible," from thinking small to thinking big. I needed to release past failures and current excuses. I was sick and tired of all those little thoughts creeping into my subconscious. Thoughts telling me I wasn't good enough. Worries about what if this happened, what if that happened? Thoughts telling me I wasn't going to succeed. That negative, nagging voice went on and on and on. I had to change it. I had to shift from allowing those thoughts to control me, to controlling my own mindset.

Here is how I started. During my entire first year, I walked around repeating to myself over and over, "I can, I will, I am. I can, I will, I am. I can, I will, I am." I lived in that mantra, saying it constantly in my mind – and sometimes it wasn't just in my mind. Sometimes I moved through the day saying aloud, "I can, I will, I am. I can, I will, I am."

Through the mentorship I had from both Bob and Craig, I knew early on that success in this business at the highest levels involves more than doing the daily activities of sharing products and business opportunities, and following up. If I wanted to build a large organization that would last, I had to create the right thoughts and feelings behind my actions. It's not just about the actions. The actions are five percent. All the training your corporate company gives you is the five percent of it. Ninety-five percent of enduring success is the mindset, the thoughts, the feelings *behind* the actions you're taking.

At some point in your business, the clichés you're taught – "Be here a year from now" and "Just keep showing up" – are not enough. If you want to become a leader, you have to move past just showing up and into molding yourself into the type of person capable of leading a team.

In addition to my "I can, I will, I am" mantra, I obsessively listened to Jim Rohn's CD *Building Your Network Marketing Business.* For the first year of my business, it was the only thing that played in my car. I absorbed every piece of that short (under an hour) CD. I learned what this business is really about. I learned it's a "do and then learn" business. It's not a "learn and then do" business. I learned "not to get distracted by little things." I learned how to "discipline my disappointments." I learned how to think like a leader, like a network marketing professional.

Liz Hartke versus her beliefs. I love sharing stories about Liz, one of my business partners. Speaking of which, I refer to a person I work with as a "partner" rather than "one of my distributors" or "somebody on my team." Leaders never want to be "one of your distributors" or on "your team." Leaders want to be partners with you, want to run a team with you, and eventually want to flourish on their own.

Okay, back to Liz. I have so enjoyed watching the work she's done and how she's grown – in her business, as a wife and mother, daughter, sister, and as a mentor and leader. I had the opportunity to play a small role in her growth and then got out of the way to watch as Liz soared to the highest levels in our company. Early in her business, she had a major breakthrough in her mindset. In our company we have a rank called "2-Star Diamond," which Liz had set herself the goal of achieving by a certain date. That date was approaching, and she still needed to sign up three or four people to hit that rank. We jumped on a call, and Liz told me how disappointed she felt that she wasn't going to hit the goal she had set.

Our conversation went something like this:

Me: What do you mean you're not going to hit it?

Liz: I need four more people, and I only have three days left to do it. There's not enough time. It's just not going to happen.

Me: Okay. So what do you mean you're not going to hit it?

Liz: Well, it's impossible. I just can't do it.

Me: Stop going out there and trying to talk to people when you don't believe that it's actually possible. You have three days to hit this goal. Spend as much time as you need – even if it's the entire next two days – getting your mind right. Even if you have to pretend, get in the mindset of *believing it's possible*. If you can take it one step further, I want you to get into the mindset of *knowing* that signing up four more people is possible and *knowing* that it's going to happen.

Liz left the call reluctant but agreeing to give it a shot.

I didn't know if she was going to hit the goal or not. I knew it was 100 percent possible, but until *she* knew, it wasn't going to happen.

Liz took the advice and shifted into the right mindset. She knew without a doubt it was going to happen, and she hit the 2-Star Diamond goal she had set for herself. This success was a launching pad for Liz. She has gone on to achieve the highest rank in our company: 15-Star Diamond. That one mindset shift had enormous impact on Liz's business.

Leaders know that just plowing along when their mind isn't right does not lead to success in this business. In order to accomplish her goal, Liz spent two-thirds of her time getting her mind right, then she went out there and did the work. Once she knew it was going to happen, people were attracted to her.

4. Leaders understand they own a "big business."

Leaders in our industry know that network marketing is big business. They don't look at it as a little side gig to make some extra money here and there.

One of the best – and worst – parts of network marketing is that there's little to no barrier to entry. Most companies require a few hundred dollars to get started. Some might creep into the thousands of dollars, which is still not high compared to starting costs for most other types of business. The best part about this is that anyone can get involved. The worst part is that you've got no skin in the game. If it doesn't work out, you've just lost a little bit of money and a little bit of time. Given the low start-up cost and the opportunity being open to anyone, network marketing can mistakenly be perceived as not a "big" opportunity or a "real" type of business. Leaders understand they're building a big business.

When I first got started, I played a mind trick on myself. I looked at my business like it was a franchise. I asked myself, "What if I bought into a McDonald's franchise or some other similar type of franchise? How much would it cost me to do that?" With a bit of research I came to some rough numbers. (I was just doing this to trick myself, so exact numbers didn't matter.) Buying into a franchise would probably cost a million or more dollars, and I would probably have to come up with, say, $250,000 to get the loan to purchase the franchise. I didn't have $250,000 at that time – I was living week to week. The point of the mindset trick was to get me to treat network marketing like a big business. I asked myself, "How seriously would I take this business if I had $250,000 on the line? If the cost of failing was $250,000?" That thought changed my work ethic. It changed the way I approached this business. It added a level of urgency, of motivation. Every morning I asked myself, "How would I act today if $250,000 was on the line? If I had a ton of employees depending on me and a huge loan out there and a brick-and-mortar business? What actions would I take today? How hard would I be pushing?"

Leaders create whatever leverage they need to ensure they're treating network marketing like the big business it is.

5. Leaders set one overarching, long-term goal.

Leaders in network marketing usually have one over-arching goal.

When I first got started, I heard about our company's Million Club – when your cumulative earnings reach $1 million. I liked the idea of earning $1 million within my business over time, but I wanted more than that. I decided to go for $1 million in a year. As Jim Rohn says, "It's got a good ring to it, millionaire, $1 million a year!" That's the goal I set for myself.

As all network marketing companies do, we have various ranks and titles you can earn: Star Diamond, Elite, Premier, Top 10, Success Club, etc. Corporate sets these goals, and I strived for many of them but only if they supported my main goal of earning $1 million a year. The most important milestone on the way to my goal was finding and developing leaders, so my daily activities focused on finding and developing leaders.

What single goal will help you get the most out of your business? Not the goal that corporate wants you to hit, but the goal that is going to give you the life you want. What is the one overarching goal, that if you hit it, all the other things would fall into place? Make it a long-term goal. Make it something that requires you to become a leader in your company. After your goal is set, make sure all your daily activities are in line with that goal. If an effort is not driving you toward that one goal, don't do it. Don't chase the shiny objects. Don't go for three or four or five goals. Don't switch gears and goals every few months. Even if your goal is not to earn $1 million a year, I ask you to look at your business and decide what you want it to do for you.

6. Leaders create momentum and ride it.

Think about a time things were clicking for you – in network marketing or another area of your life. A time you were doing well at something, and you felt excited and confident about it. You were in the groove. Leaders get themselves into that grove in their business. *Success* magazine's Darren Hardy calls this the "Big Mo."

I teach my leaders that gaining momentum in this business is like surfing a big wave. In order to get out to the big wave, you have to go through the crashing surf.

Once you get through the surf, the water is calm. Then the wave comes in and, if you get on top of that wave, you're riding the energy. You're riding the momentum of that wave. Its momentum carries you forward. You're no longer crashing around in the surf and the work is not as hard because you are riding the power of the wave.

It's the same with building your business. The surf is your fears, your insecurities, your self-doubt, the negative talk going through your mind. The surf is your lack of success and your lack of skills when you're first getting started. We have to move through these pieces in order to get out to the wave. As we move through them one by one and start to see some small wins, we get closer to the wave, to the momentum. We're getting to the end of the surf and out to where we can catch a wave. And when that wave comes, that momentum is built, our job is to surf it, to ride it as best we can. Finding the momentum and riding it promotes massive growth in your business, is fun, and is much less work than crashing around in the surf.

7. Leaders give themselves permission to succeed.

So many of us are waiting for permission to become the person we're capable of becoming in this business. Right now, as you're reading, I want you to hear and I want you to feel – from my heart to yours – that you have permission to succeed at the highest levels in this business. Whenever I'm mentoring one-on-one, I always share that nobody's going to crown you king or queen in this business. If you want to be a leader in our industry, *you* are going to have to crown yourself king or queen. And until you do that, you will not see long-term success in your business. In the history of the world, there have only been two ways to become a king or queen:

1. It's in your bloodline and you inherit the title.

2. You earn the title.

In this business, no one has the bloodline of a king or queen. It doesn't matter who you signed up with, who your mentor is, what company you chose, or when you got started. Nobody's going to give you that crown. There's no inheritance in network marketing, you have to earn your title.

Action Steps

Set aside a few hours to hone in on what you are working toward in your business. Work through the following exercises in a quiet place where you won't be interrupted.

1. Referring to the action steps from the last chapter, bring back to mind the life you want to live five years from now. Write down the long-term (five-year) income goal you are going to strive for to support that life. Make that goal the center of all your daily activities. During your working hours, strive to do only those activities which support your goal.

2. Think of a short-term (three- to six-month) goal that is a stepping stone for your five-year goal. Write it down and make it your "push" goal over the next three to six months.

3. Create "I am" statements around the concept of giving yourself permission to succeed at the highest levels in your business. An "I am" statement is simply a powerful, positive affirmation starting with "I am." Create 10-20 statements to roll around in your mind throughout the day. Examples:
   - I am becoming a leader of leaders.
   - I am empowered.
   - I am confident.

Chapter 4

BUILD TO LAST AND YOUR PERSONAL DEVELOPMENT PLAN

As a leader, it's a major responsibility on your shoulders to practice the behavior you want others to follow.
— Himanshu Bhatia

Don't Mistake Information Gathering for Personal Development

Most of us have a major misconception about personal development. We think personal development is something you just sit down and do. Read 10 pages a day. Listen to the podcast on your ride to work. Jump on the training call. This, however, is just information gathering, which is useless if we don't do anything with it. It's not personal development. Personal development is the combination of those two words. You're *developing* yourself as a *person*, a process that involves understanding "who you are" right now and "who you need to be" in order to achieve your goals and dreams.

Most distributors fall short by focusing on "what are the activities that I have to do?" *Leaders* focus on "who is the person I need to become in order to build the team I want?" Once you get clear on who you are and who you need to be, you can then look for the resources to close the gap. And here is the important part: you need to do more than study and learn, you need to *implement*. You need to *become!* It's not an information-gathering plan, it's a personal-development plan.

"52 Books a Year" Is Not a Personal Development Plan

One day on a private Facebook page for leaders in the company I work with, I read a post by a leader who had committed to reading 52 books during the year, along with a few of his team members. Many people commented on the book-a-week post – "exciting," "great idea." I couldn't disagree more. (Don't get me wrong, I'm a book junkie. I probably skim 52 books in a year and deep dive into a few that are relevant to my growth at the time, but I don't read just to read.) Looking at that thread, I wondered, "How much is somebody actually going to learn, and how much more are they going to become? How will they implement what they learn if they just read book after book after book?"

When I work on personal development with people I mentor, we find the areas in their life – in their character, their self-esteem, their leadership – where they want to grow. Then we find resources for those specific spots, and they work on improving.

For example, you're reading this book. You can plow through it and gain a lot of new information. But if you don't *implement* what you're reading, you're not going to become who you want to become. Consuming information gets you nowhere. To use this book effectively, after reading it, you'll put little pieces of it to work for you. You do this step by step. You take the good – the aspects that you need – and discard the rest. Just gaining some information isn't enough. Taking that information and applying it to your life – that's a personal development plan.

Your Personal Development Plan Is Not Limited

I used to be a massive consumer of information, reading personal development books until two o'clock in the morning. But I wasn't necessarily applying what I learned. I was gaining information, but my life wasn't changing. When I turned 25, it became clear to me that I needed a therapist. My life wasn't working. I was not happy, I was depressed, I was having anxiety and panic attacks all the time. I didn't know what to do anymore. I truly needed help.

I met with four therapists before I found one who clicked with me, who spoke truth into my life. She wasn't there to comfort or coddle me. For a year, I went to her every week for an hour and then implemented everything she told me to during the following week. I did the work. I wasn't just consuming information anymore. I took action on everything she assigned me. Do you see the difference between just gathering information and actually engaging in personal development?

Your Personal Development Plan

Let's begin right now. Grab a pen and paper (or come back to this section later), and let's put together your personal development plan as it relates to your network marketing business. Start by jotting down the leaders in your company and leaders you admire, then list qualities you admire in those leaders. Most likely, you'll identify many different leadership qualities – from technical leadership skills to self-esteem to how they make others feel. You may admire somebody for her ability to inspire others. You may admire another person for the duplicatable systems he created for his team. You may admire yet another leader for the way he always brings in top-quality people or for his trustworthy character. How do those leaders inspire their team and how do those leaders make the individuals on their team feel? Put your inventory of these qualities into a list.

You've just defined your idea of the pinnacle of leadership, in other words, who you're looking to become. This is *your ideal self* as a leader in network marketing.

Now it's time to take an honest gut check: where are you right now? Rate yourself on a scale of 1 to 10 for each of the qualities you're looking to grow into. Get a clear understanding of where you are today and where you want to be. You take the inventory so you can see the gap. Once you see the gap, you know where you need to improve. Your improvement plan covers the distance between where you currently are and where you want to be.

How to Bridge the Gap

How do you bridge that gap? To paraphrase Wayne Dyer, it doesn't matter what you're *willing* to do. People are willing to do a lot. They're willing to sacrifice a lot. I'm sure you too have been willing to give a lot, do a lot, and sacrifice a lot. But the real question, again paraphrasing Wayne Dyer, is "What's the piece that you're not willing to do?" When you figure out what's on your "I'm not willing to do that" list, you're well on your way to putting together your personal development plan.

If you want success at the highest level, you have to get your "I'm not willing to do that" list as close as possible to zero. It's always the place you don't want to go – the things you don't want to admit that you need to address. That you need to improve. That you need to work through. That fear, that doubt, that insecurity, that depression, that "I'm not good enough" self-talk, that piece you've been carrying with you since childhood. Whatever that is, get clear about those places you don't want to go, those things you don't want to do, because that's where real change and growth occurs.

Once you know what you need to start working on, find the right resources to help you. Find people who have been there, who have done it before you. Model them. What is it that they've done? How have they gone through it? How have they reinvented themselves? You may hire a mentor or a virtual mentor. Maybe it's your sponsor. It doesn't necessarily have to be someone you work with one-on-one, although it can be. Your resources may be books, CDs, courses, success partners, someone to model. You may get a therapist. There are so many possibilities. I wish there were a checklist or formula, but this process is different for everyone.

If there *were* a formula, it would be a simple one:

> Where are you now?
> Where do you want to go?
> Create a plan to bridge the gap.

Two Guidelines

Here are two guidelines to be aware of as you put together your plan:

1. Make sure the person you choose to work with, to model, to use as a resource, has what you want or has done what you want to do. Some "mentors" are strong presenters but haven't actually achieved what you're setting out to.

2. While you're working on your personal development plan, make sure you're also working on your

business. We're in a "do and then learn business." Let me repeat that. Network marketing is a "do and then learn business." So get out there. Take the action. Do it even when you're scared. That's the way you learn how to do it a little better next time. Don't wait for the timing to be "perfect." It's okay to be uncomfortable. Know your action creates positive energy that trumps your fears, your insecurities, your doubts – and builds self-esteem – making it easier to take the action next time.

Action Steps

1. If you have not yet done so, make a list of all the positive qualities of the leaders you admire. To help you with this assignment, you can refer to the section of this chapter titled "Your Personal Development Plan." You can also refer to the first Action Step in Chapter 2.

2. On a scale of 1 to 10, rate yourself on each of the positive qualities you admire in other leaders.

3. Given your list of qualities and your current rating, reflect on the long-term and short-term goals you put together in the last chapter. With those goals in mind, what three qualities, if improved, will have the biggest positive impact on the achievement of your goals?

4. Take immediate action (today) on each of the three improvement areas you identified above. Keep it simple. Just take the first step – it could be making a phone call, making a list, setting an appointment, buying a book. Then continue to take daily action in the same manner.

Chapter 5

BUILD TO LAST AND YOUR BELIEF

A genuine leader is not a searcher
for consensus but a molder of consensus.
—Martin Luther King, Jr.

Get Out of Your Own Way

For new distributors and even seasoned distributors, one of the biggest obstacles to building a large organization is not recognizing the value of what you have to offer. The opportunity you have can change lives, and people are looking for what you have to offer. But we can be hesitant to approach friends, acquaintances, and strangers for fear of bothering them. We don't want to continue to follow up for fear of pestering or pressuring. We feel like we're always trying to push our business opportunity or products on other people.

Have you ever felt that way? Do you feel that way right now?

It's a block to building a large organization. Heck, it's a block to getting your business off the ground. So take the step of recognizing and embracing the value of the opportunity of network marketing. Recognize the impact this business can have on someone's life. Recognize that people are literally dying to be understood, heard, validated. They are sick and tired of being sick and tired. People are looking for an opportunity, but most distributors are caught up in worrying about what others think and miss the chance to serve.

A Helping Hand Can Save Someone

Often, when I share this story, the enormity of the opportunity of network marketing "clicks."

I was driving along in my truck, with two of my kids in the back seat, listening to Tara Brach's podcast when this story about two high school boys came up. The story was told in the first person, so that's how I'll tell it here. It goes something like this:

I was putting my books away and closing up my locker when I noticed this new boy who had just come to our school. We were about two weeks into my freshman year. I hadn't seen him before, and I noticed he was really disheveled looking. As I'm glancing over, I see that he's trying to get books out of his locker. He's got an armful of books ready to fall, and a few that have already fallen on the floor. I decided to help him, which was out of character for me. I walked over and bent down to pick up a few books from the floor. I was on one knee, and the new boy was standing up, and I reached up to him and handed him a book. He was looking down at me with these eyes. I had never seen anybody look at me with eyes like that before.

The eyes were deeper than a normal thank you. Through his eyes and into my heart, into my soul, an inner voice said, "Thank you for doing that." I grabbed the other books and handed them to him. We started chatting a little bit, and I learned his name was Steven. Steven had just come to our school from another school. We talked for a while and then decided to walk home together, which was also out of character for me. It turned out we live a couple of houses down the road from each other. This walk home together became a routine. We started walking to and from school together, and eventually we became good friends.

Fast forward to senior year. I had watched this boy turn into a man. Steven was the valedictorian of our class. He was also the prom king and the star athlete on our football team. He had a beautiful girlfriend. He was the kindest, most sincere, genuine person I knew. I envied him for the guy he was and the life he was living. I was also grateful to be his closest friend.

Now it's graduation and we're in the auditorium. As valedictorian, Steven's about to give the commencement speech. I'm sitting behind him. I can see that he's really nervous. I put my arm on his shoulder and tell him he's going to do a great job, that everything's going to be perfect, that he has so much to offer the students. He turns around while my arm is on his shoulder and looks me in the eyes with that same look he had given me during our freshman year when I picked up the books for him, and I felt it again. I felt that thank you that penetrates deeper than a normal thank you.

They call up Steven as valedictorian and I can't wait to hear what he has to say. He starts his speech talking about high school. How high school is a time when we have these different people in our lives who impact us. We have our parents, and he goes into the impact they have on us. Then he talks about our teachers and how we had so many amazing teachers at the school and the role that they played in shaping our minds and helping us to vision and create an idea of who we want to become.

"But you know what the most important thing is?" he says. "The most important relationships we have during our high school years are with our friends. I never want you to underestimate the power of simply caring about somebody, of performing a kind act

and not worrying about yourself, not worrying about what others are going to think. When I first moved to this school, you were already two weeks into the school year and I had just left another school because of the amount of teasing and bullying I had to endure there. I got picked on to the point that I couldn't stay anymore. My parents moved us, and I started school here. My first day here, the bullying started again. I decided that I had had enough. At the end of the day I decided to clear out my locker. I was going to commit suicide that day, and I didn't want my parents to have another thing to deal with. I figured if I cleared out my locker, it was one less thing they would have to handle.

"As I was clearing out my locker, I was shaking and I was nervous and I kept dropping my books. Somebody came over, bent down, picked up some of those books and handed them to me. In that moment I felt hope. I felt love. I felt like I might just be able to figure out how to belong. That one act of kindness and caring got me through the day. That one act of kindness started a journey which took me from who I was four years ago — the insecure, depressed, anxious kid who was about to commit suicide — to where I am today. I want you to remember, when you go out there in the world, that we all need someone. We all need someone to lend a helping hand. We all need someone who cares. And finally, remember that you're never going to know who is really in need, so just make it a habit of leading with kindness and offering a helping hand when you can."

You're Offering a Gift

I was sitting there listening to this story and bawling. My two children were in the back of the truck wondering, "What's going on with Papa?" I was floored by this story. I immediately saw it as the missing piece for so many in our business. The network marketing industry has the ability to save lives. Don't think otherwise. People living paycheck to paycheck, getting their car repossessed, defaulting on their mortgage, people who aren't connecting with their family because they're exhausted and don't have the time – they need a way to get out of the pressure of their job. In situations like these, network marketing can offer the ability to take back your life. Take back your time. Gain the freedom to do what you want, when you want, with who you want. That's the opportunity we offer. That's what this business is about. What we offer is a gift that can change somebody's life dramatically. It happened for me. It has happened for so many people I've mentored. And it has been happening for over 100 years in our industry. Network marketing is a proven model to take back your life! Take the step of accepting that gift, and start sharing it as a *gift* – not as something you're trying to sell someone to hit the next goal your company set out for you.

What if you start looking at your network marketing business that way? Instead of "I don't want to message them. I don't know if they're going to want this. They might make fun of me. They might ignore me. They might be turned off." What if you start approaching others knowing you have a gift? What if you approached the day looking for every opportunity to share this gift? See the difference? Can you make that shift right now? You have to understand the biggest obstacle to your success is you, it's you and your own limiting beliefs. Let them go. Receive this gift and then gift it to others. Our business IS that simple.

Visualize Your Highest Good

When I start mentoring new people, they're often unfamiliar with the practice of visualization, a tool used by high achievers in all arenas. Visualization is simply seeing what you want *in your mind* before it comes into being. Research has shown that actually shooting basketball free throws and *visualizing* the practice of shooting free throws are equally effective in improving performance. It's scientifically proven, visualization works!

I start people by inviting them to visualize their ultimate goal. What will it feel like when you achieve it? Who will you have become? What changes will you have made in your life? What will you have had to grow through? To see these successes in material form in your business, first you have to see them within your mind through your visualization practice. You focus on seeing it and experiencing it and believing it. Your "vision" gets into your heart and soul, and then starts appearing in your life.

My personal sponsor Bob's goal was to have 10,000 distributors. That's what he was visualizing when he first started and didn't even have 100 distributors yet. He had no idea how he was going to get there. He didn't know the steps he would have to take. He couldn't even believe it in his mind, yet somehow deep inside of him he knew it was possible. And he kept visualizing, kept praying, kept holding that dream until it became a reality.

My vision for this business was to make $1 million a year. Crazy goal because I had never made more than $100,000 a year in my life. I had no idea *how* it was possible. My mind couldn't conceive of it. But somewhere inside of me, I knew it was possible. I focused on seeing it, focused on believing it, and eventually came to *know* that it was going to happen. That knowing seemed to act like a magnetic power attracting success to me.

"Can I Do This?" Is the Wrong Question

Most people who intend to build a large organization roll around in their mind questions like these: "Can I do this?" "Do I have what it takes?" "Is this going to work for me?" "Am I wasting my time?" Those are the wrong questions. The right question for you to ask is: "Am I willing to do what it takes to become the person I need to become?" The reality is that you can't do it right now as you are. You can't do it with your current level of skills. If you could, you would already be there and not be reading this book. Once you shift the question that's repeating in your mind to "Am I willing to do what it takes?" and you answer "Yes," here's where you live: "I can, I will, I am. I can, I will, I am. I can, I will, I am." Repeat that over and over. Keep seeing it, believing it, taking daily action, until you know with certainty that your dream is coming to fruition.

You've Had Your Sign-Up Date But Have You Had Your Birth Date?

My mentor Craig Holiday shared this with me: everybody in network marketing who achieves success has both a sign-up date and a birth date. Two totally different things. Your *sign-up date* is when you sign up to become a network marketer. Your *birth date* is when you actually give birth to this business. The business comes alive, starts forming, starts growing, then – just like a baby – the business is born!

So many people only have a sign-up date and never have a birth date. They don't arrive at that point of being willing to do whatever it takes (as long as it's aligned with their morals) to be successful in this business. For people who arrive at that birth date, everything starts to click. Network marketing becomes really, really fun. To quote Craig, "Building it fast is fun, but building it slow sucks."

Getting into the Knowing Space

When I first got started with my business, sometimes I couldn't sleep when I got into bed at night. I was both excited and overwhelmed by introducing this business opportunity and helping others. Sometimes I dreamed about lots of people coming to me to sign up *before* lots of people actually started coming. I remember a conversation around that time with Craig, who excels at planting a vision in your heart and your mind.

Craig: Keith, when it happens for you, when it really happens and that first million comes in, how are you going to react?

Me: I honestly don't think it's going to be a big deal.

Craig: What do you mean?

Me: I know it's going to happen, Craig. There isn't an ounce of doubt in me. It's almost like it's already happened.

That shows you my level of belief.

That's where I want *you* to get.

How do you get there? By constant, obsessive visualization and dreaming. You visualize what you want every single day, where you're going, the person you're becoming. There are many practices you can implement for this: write down your vision in the morning, have a prayer with it, carry note cards with you, set a reminder on your phone that goes off every hour, make a dream board, put messages around the house on mirrors, on your refrigerator, anywhere you'll see them over and over. Figure out what works for you.

Visualize what you want, and let go of what you don't want.

Yes, negative thoughts will creep in – thoughts like "It's not going to happen," "It's impossible," "Who do you think you are?" It's okay for those thoughts to arise, but it's not okay for you to allow those thoughts to attach to you.

Action Step

Spend quiet time rolling around the following ideas in your mind until they become real for you and you start acting from that knowing:

What I have to offer is a gift, not a burden. I've made the decision to let go of any fear of approaching others with my opportunity. I know our industry has the ability to change the lives of those who join and the generations who follow.

Section Two

LEADING OTHERS

"Leading Others" lays out what you have to do to attract, identify, and eventually mentor leaders.

You will learn how to attract other leaders by using sequential positioning techniques so you are seen as an authority from the start. You will learn the two questions that go through every prospect's subconscious mind and how to always be answering those questions. You will learn the two forces that move people to action in our business. You will learn several ways to "funnel" and "filter" distributors in your downline allowing you to focus your attention on those who have leadership potential and are motivated to grow. You will learn, step by step, how to mentor leaders. You will learn the importance of building trust with those you mentor and how to build that trust. You will learn how to push those you are mentoring past their limiting beliefs and through their fears. You will learn my bridge system for walking leaders through each step of their development. Finally, you will learn what to do when one of your leaders no longer needs you.

Chapter 6

POSITIONING YOURSELF
AS A LEADER

I am not afraid of an army of lions led by a sheep;
I am afraid of an army of sheep led by a lion.
— Alexander the Great

You Must Be Seen as a Leader from the Start

To build a team of leaders, you must position yourself in the eyes of others as a leader from your initial contact, not just when you start working with them. When you are recruiting, people have to see you as a leader, which involves conveying to everyone you come across in this business that you know what you're doing and where you're going, and you're offering an invitation to come along.

When I signed up as a distributor, I went all in and talked to everybody I knew about the business opportunity.

I shared in a simple but passionate way: "I just got

signed up as a distributor with XYZ Company, not sure if you've heard of them before, but it's something I'm going to run with 100 percent. Would you be willing to check this out? You don't have to commit to it or sign up, but please just check it out."

That's all I said to the first thousand or so people I talked to. I didn't do anything more than that.

Here is the difference maker: when I approached others about joining me in this business, they saw me as a leader they could follow right from the start.

Steps to Getting Others to See You as a Leader from the Start

1. Approach people with faith, enthusiasm, and action.
2. Present a once-in-a-lifetime opportunity.
3. Position yourself as the one in charge, as the leader.

Approach Your Business with Faith, Enthusiasm, and Action

I give credit to my personal sponsor, Bob, for sharing with me with those three words: faith, enthusiasm, and action. "Go out and do your work with the power of faith, enthusiasm, and action behind all your business-building efforts," he said.

Faith in yourself and your business. Faith in your product. Faith in the ability of multilevel marketing to work for you. Faith in the vision you're building. Faith that you can build this with or without any potential distributor. That's a huge piece. There's nothing worse than chasing people down and feeling you *need* them to sign up. There's nothing better than their knowing you would love to work with them, but you don't need them.

Enthusiasm is like a magic wand. You can't directly measure it, but people can feel when you do your work enthusiastically. You're enthusiastically talking to people.

You're enthusiastically sharing the business opportunity. You're enthusiastically communicating the vision of where you're going. It's been said that sales is simply *a transference of energy and belief from one person to the other.* When you know where you're going, when people can feel the energy you have, when they can feel your enthusiasm about your opportunity, you pass that on to them. Your enthusiasm becomes part of them. They become enthusiastic alongside you.

Action is simply going out there and doing the work. Showing up every single day, putting in the hours, week after week, month after month, year after year.

Position yourself as a leader by approaching your business with faith, enthusiasm, and action.

Present a Once-in-a-lifetime Opportunity

Looking back, I recognize that whenever my business experienced jumps in volume or emerging leaders, we were always focused on something big. A Big-New-Exciting Opportunity in the business right now that people could not miss out on. Something exclusive right here, right now.

Here are a few approaches I've used to present this business as a once-in-a-lifetime opportunity:

1. Ground Floor – When I first got started, my company was already five years old, but I promoted this being a ground-floor opportunity for my first year.

2. New Training Coming Up – I just revamped my training, and this is an exclusive, test-group launch of the new training. I'm looking for a few new distributors to mentor.

3. New Face to the Company – We just partnered with an investment company that infused $50 million into our infrastructure. Ride this new growth.

4. New Product Release – There's a new product coming out, now is the time to get in.

5. New Territory – We're expanding into a new country and looking for partners there.

That's an abridged list, but you get the idea. When you go out there and talk about your business – whether one-on-one, on social media, or wherever else you're sharing – your emphasis is always about your next new, big thing. This special situation is coming up, and you're looking for partners to join you.

As partners start coming into your "next big thing," you want to celebrate it and make it public in your social media, emails, etc. I love the whole process of celebrating. It's fun and it builds momentum. I say things like, "We've got this new training, only 30 spots available. Oh, 2 spots taken! So-and-so signed up and so-and-so signed up. Oh, 2 more spots taken – so-and-so signed up and so-and-so signed up." Then the people watching are thinking, "Oh, wow. That person from work signed up." It creates a buzz around your big opportunity. That buzz leads those who are on the fence and watching, to reach out to you.

Position Yourself as the One in Charge

To position yourself as the one in charge, *you* need to know and *others* need to know that you don't need them. I know it sounds harsh. It's not that you don't want to work with them. You would love to work with them. There's nothing more that you want, but you don't need them. You have something to offer that they need. See yourself as a leader. Position yourself as the one in charge.

When someone is interested in signing up with me, I use four tools to position myself as the one in charge:

1. An application.
2. A follow-up phone or video interview.
3. A welcome email.
4. A "getting started right" call.

The Application

Have people fill out your application regardless of how they come to you. Don't just send them your sign-up link. If you've been out talking to somebody face-to-face and she decides she's interested in working with you, your next step is sending her an application. If you've been posting on social media, someone is watching, and he's ready to sign up, your next step is to send him an application. Your long-term goal is building leaders in your downline. The application is part of the positioning process. Don't skip it because you want to rush to sign people up.

When people have to fill out an application before talking with me, what did I just do? I positioned myself. Now, they're coming to me. They're filling out an application to work with me. Some of the application questions are designed to give me an understanding of what people want to get out of this business. Are they looking to do a little part-time thing or are they looking to build a big business? If they're looking to build a big business, are they willing to see me as a mentor? Are they willing to have an employee-employer relationship? Are they willing to put together a personal development plan? Are they going to be coachable?

After they fill out the application, an email auto-responder directs them to text me so I know they sent an application in.

BONUS Application and auto-responder available at *www.KeithCallahan.com/book*.

Again, you see the positioning? People fill out an application. The application asks a bunch of questions and positions me as the authority. Then they get an email back saying, "I'm super busy, send me a text message so I know to check for your application." From the start these steps set a tone and expectation regarding how our relationship will work.

The Interview

Many big-time recruiters do not see the value in the interview and skip it. Don't do that. If you're looking to build a long-term sustainable business, you want to start developing relationships with the people in your downline (which we'll explore in detail in a later chapter).

During the interview with a potential distributor, my goal is to make sure we're a fit for each other. My willingness to spend half an hour with somebody who hasn't signed up yet gives me leverage because many other distributors are not willing to get on the phone with a prospect. Doing so says a lot. It also starts our relationship-building process.

BONUS 12-minute audio and accompanying PDF detailing this interview process available at
www.KeithCallahan.com/book.

The Welcome Email

When new distributors sign up, I send them a welcome email with two attachments: a checklist and a questionnaire. The checklist sets up new people to succeed by taking action right away. It also gives me the opportunity to stress what I think is important, not what corporate thinks is important. Corporate is not focused on building leaders, therefore, their welcome email is likely to be very different from my welcome email.

Much of what we work on initially is getting a new distributor's mind in the right place, not navigating the back-end office, how to set up their website, and the like. My focus is on the big picture, on inspiring, on getting distributors oriented toward my thinking.

The questionnaire helps me better understand who they are and what their goals are. It's similar to the application they already filled out, but more detailed. I then work with their questionnaire responses on our "getting started right" call.

The welcome email and attachments represent quite a bit of work for new distributors. If they do all of it, they're really diving in. They're thinking about their goals. They're thinking about how they want to start building their business. All of this positions me as an authority and at the same time focuses them in the right direction, and generates enthusiasm and excitement about what is coming.

BONUS Welcome email with checklist and questionnaire available at *www.KeithCallahan.com/book*.

The "Getting Started Right" Call

Finally we arrive at the "getting started right" call. By this time the distributor's attitude is: "Keith, tell me exactly what to do." She has this attitude because of how I've positioned our relationship from the start. Consider the process she has gone through: as a prospective new distributor, she fills out an application, then has a phone call in which I explain how I mentor and what she can expect; she signs up, and her welcome email gives her 10 things to do and another questionnaire. All this positions me as the authority. Collectively it says, "I know what I'm doing. I'm completely capable of helping you achieve your goals, and I'm going to show you what to do, step by step." This allows me to set expectations from the outset.

BONUS 11-minute audio and accompanying PDF detailing this call available at
www.KeithCallahan.com/book.

One of the questions distributors I mentor ask frequently is "How do you get your distributors working right away?" As you can see, I don't sign up distributors and *then* tell them, "Okay, now it's time to get to work."

The entire getting-started process indicates: I'm going to work, it's going to be uncomfortable, but Keith is going to set goals and show me exactly what to do right from the start. So when distributors sign up with me, they're nervous – just like all new distributors – but they take action right away. They take action because they have been expected to all along. When I start new distributors, they're usually signing up people within the first day. The first week at the longest. That's what I expect. Because I expect it and because I have positioned myself as the authority, that's the only path they know.

Can you see how adhering to this process positions you as a leader? Can you see how this positioning influences the way new distributors start their business? Leading others and getting them started strong doesn't begin when they sign up. It begins with being a leader from the first interaction.

Action Steps

1. Download my templates at
www.KeithCallahan.com/book to use in creating your
own scripts and documents:
   a)   An application for interested prospects.
   b)   A follow-up email for that application.
   c)   Your interview script.
   d)   Your welcome email.

2. Go through the last few weeks of your recruiting
content (what you've put on social media) and think
about the conversations you have had. Do the people
you're interacting with see you as a leader? Is that the
message you're conveying? If not, make the commitment to shift what you say and share.

Chapter 7

ATTRACTING LEADERS

*Leadership is the ability to guide others without force
into a direction or decision that leaves them still feeling
empowered and accomplished.*
— Lisa Cash Hanson

Attracting leaders is 100 percent about you. It's not about your products, services, or business opportunity. People are buying YOU. Think about it like you're a magnet looking to attract that perfect prospect. Whatever means you use (face-to-face, email, social media, etc.), the more attractive you are, the more magnetic you are, the more people are going to be drawn to you. People are buying your energy, your story, your vision, your dream. People are attracted to you, follow you, and eventually become a partner of yours because they're inspired by who you are and what you stand for.

Questions Every Prospect Asks

Two questions will go through the mind of every prospect you come across, though they never ask you directly:

1. Does [your name here] have the ability to help me achieve my goals?

2. Can I do this?

These two questions are like the first domino in a series of dominos. If you can answer these two questions, all their other questions and reservations become irrelevant. You will speak to these two questions over and over as you're out there recruiting.

Does he or she have the ability to help me achieve my goals? The more magnetic you are, the more you believe in yourself, the more you know where you're going, the clearer your vision and your dream, the more your prospect will know you have the ability to help her get where she wants to go. At this point in your reading of *Build to Last*, you know that if you sign up with me, I have the ability to mentor you in achieving your goals. Why? Because I've positioned myself that way.

Can I do this? We all need someone to believe in us, and you can offer that belief in your prospect that he CAN actually do this. Whenever I talk to a prospect, I highlight qualities I see in him and how those qualities will contribute to his success in this business.

If he knows you have the ability to help him achieve his goals and he believes he can do it, you've empowered him to succeed.

A Period of Imbalance

Attracting leaders requires enormous energy. Making a real run at your network marketing business takes massive imbalance upfront. It needs to become an obsession, the only thing you think about, for a period of time. The best way for me to describe this is by sharing how it was for me in the beginning.

When I made the decision to start my network marketing business, I also made the decision to go all in. I let go of everything else in my life except two things: my family and this business. That's all I focused on for an entire year. I stopped watching TV. I stopped going out with friends. I even stopped spending time with my extended family, except for holidays. I was obsessed with this business. It was my burning obsession because IT HAS TO BE.

To succeed at the highest levels in our industry, you first have to "get the boulder over the hill." Getting the boulder over the hill is getting your business to the point that it starts to run away from you. When you attract other leaders and they start building their business, eventually your business thrives with or without you. Getting the boulder over the hill is when your team is producing exponentially more than you personally are producing. But *you* have to get that boulder over the hill, which takes massive imbalance and energy in the beginning.

For that first year I had an agreement with my wife. She understood that we were going to have imbalance for a while. If anybody tells you that you can put in five hours a week and it's just going to build and build, they're wrong. Building to last doesn't work that way. You might experience small success that way, but if you want big success, you have to get that boulder over the hill. If you're in the process of getting the boulder over the hill and you stop for even a week, that boulder will roll back down the hill. The longer you stop, the further down the hill the boulder rolls. If you're halfway up the hill and you stop doing the work for a month or so, the boulder rolls all the way back down and you've got to start over again.

During This Period of Imbalance, Set Your Soul on Fire

My mentor, Craig, loved sharing a particular story about the energy and mindset you have to get yourself into to get the boulder over the hill and succeed with this business. The story goes like this:

You're on the highway driving home from work one day. You've been driving for a while and you're nearing your exit. You see lights flashing and pull over to the shoulder. A bunch of fire trucks rush past you, sirens blowing. They're flying down the highway, fire truck after fire truck. It concerns you. What could be going on? Obviously not something good. And it looks like they're heading to the town you live in. All the trucks go by, and you get back on the highway then take your exit. Now you start to get a little more concerned because as you get off the main road and turn down the street toward your home, you realize all the fire trucks are heading that way. You get even more concerned when you realize they're going toward your house. As you turn the corner toward your home, you see all the trucks are at your house because it's on fire! You speed up, arrive at the house, get out of your car, and start walking toward the house.

One of the fire fighters puts out an arm and says to you, "You can't go in there."

You respond, "That's my house!"

The fire fighter says, "I know, but you can't go in there. The house is on fire. It's not safe for you to go in there."

You sink down, totally deflated, and realize your entire house with all your memories in it is about to burn to the ground.

That's one way the story could go. Here is a second way:

You're driving home and getting off the highway. As you exit, you see fire trucks going by and realize they're taking a left.

They're going down toward your house. Again you're getting nervous, thinking, "Whoa, what's going on?" Your heart starts beating a little faster. You drive a bit further and see the fire trucks taking a right into the cul-de-sac where your house is. Now your heart really starts racing, and then you realize it's your house on fire! You step on the gas. You're trembling and shaking and crying and screaming. You go speeding into your yard and park right on the grass – the car coming to a skidding halt. You jump out of the car, slam the door, and run toward the house. A fire fighter tries to stop you, but this time you push past him and three other fire fighters. Nobody is going to stop you from getting into that burning house. Nothing is going to hold you back because your family is inside that house!

You run up there, risking your own life. Nothing else matters in this moment. Nothing is going to stand in the way of your getting in that house and rescuing your family. You're utterly focused. Nothing else enters your mind, nothing else matters at this moment. You have one job: rescue your family.

When you start going after your dreams like you would go after your family in that burning house – with that energy – that's when you start attracting people into this business. Many of us need to move through the energy level of seeing a house on fire and saying, "Oh, bummer," to the intensity of saving your family.

How I Got My Mind Right

I want to share with you how I got my mind right using a combination of elements including morning and evening rituals. First thing in the morning, I walked to an altar space I had set up to make a prayer of gratitude for two things: the ten people I was going to be able to talk to about this business today, and the two people who were actually going to sit down and go through a business presentation with me. Then I went about my day, seeking those opportunities. All day, my mind, heart, and energy – my whole being – was looking for those people I could talk with. I was excited to encounter the two people who would sit down with me to delve into this business. And every single day, I was able to engage in ten conversations and every single day, I was able to present the business twice.

If I started to lose my energy and excitement, I used to bounce up and down, doing this little dance, saying to myself, "Funk, funk, funk. Get out of that funk." I would do my no-rhythm, white-man body-bop to get back in the energy of my morning prayer of gratitude. I would repeat my mantra: "I can, I will, I am. I can, I will, I am." Then I would get back in action and start talking to people. That's where I lived during that whole first year. Aligning (and realigning) my energy and taking action.

At the end of each day, I offered gratitude. In my evening ritual, I returned to my altar, giving thanks for the people I was able to talk to and for the two business presentations I was able to make.

It Takes Six Months to See Results

When you get to this point in your business, be prepared for it to take roughly six months before you start seeing the results. They don't come overnight. You have to hold strong and focus on "doing" before you start seeing the results. You have to see it and believe it and know it before it actually happens. And you have to have patience. Then, it's about *doing*. It's about talking to more and more people, staying in action, massive imbalance for a finite period. Get that boulder over the hill until you have so many leaders in your business, so many new distributors coming in every month that it doesn't matter what YOU do. Your leaders and team are going to have a much larger impact than you because of the foundation you laid. That's where you're going.

Action Step

This chapter's single action step is a big one.

Make an honest list of the time-consuming activities in your life that don't contribute to your future. Commit to one year of imbalance. Give up those things and focus strictly on your business.

Chapter 8

IDENTIFYING LEADERS

I was never top of the class at school,
but my classmates must have seen potential in me,
because my nickname was "Einstein."
— Stephen Hawking

Not Everyone Is a Leader

Once you're able to identify potential leaders, you can start working with them to develop them into the leaders they're meant to be. Recognize that everybody you sponsor is not going to become a leader. Not everybody is meant to be a leader. Some are not capable, some are capable but don't want to become leaders, and some are capable but not yet ready to lead.

I cannot stress enough that you can't force someone into something he is not ready for or capable of. That's like trying to force someone to quit an addiction when he's not ready to do it himself. You can point him in the right direction and talk about the destruction his habit is bringing upon himself and others. But until a person is ready to get help, you can't help him.

One of the most common situations new leaders ask me about is: "How do I get my distributors to the next level?" In fact, the majority of distributors are never going to get to the next level, no matter what you do. They're not all going to become leaders.

This is how multilevel marketing works: instead of trying to change the probabilities and force action on those who are never going to become leaders, your approach is to work the numbers.

Working the Numbers

Here's how I look at the numbers. If you recruit 100 people, 30 to 50 of them are going to do something. Those who actually do something might sign up one or a few customers, or they might sign up a few distributors. Of the 30 to 50 who actually do something, perhaps 3 will become leaders.

When you're first getting started, you don't have 100 people to sift through to find your three leaders, so you'll work with anybody who signs up with you as though that person is a leader. I work with my leaders one-on-one. When you first become a distributor and start bringing in other distributors, you work one-on-one with everybody you bring in. Eventually, given the number of people in your team, you can only work with the leaders one-on-one and everyone else in a group. That's where you want to get. You want so many people coming into your business that you have to identify the leaders and spend most of your "team building" time with your real, running leaders.

How to Know You Have a Leader

How do I know that someone in my downline is a potential leader? There's no specific type of person who is going to become a leader in your business. A leader could be a doctor, a lawyer, a janitor, a teacher, a recovering alcoholic, a stay-at-home mom, a model citizen, a high-school dropout...Leaders come from all different backgrounds and have all different personality types. However, specific character traits do appear over and over in leaders. They're self-motivated. They're solution-oriented. They're problem solvers. They're competitive. They're usually busy in the rest of their lives. They believe in something bigger than themselves. They're action-oriented. They're dreamers. They're coachable. They're motivated by either inspiration or desperation. And also, they inspire me.

In that list of traits, the last two stand out for me as important identifiers.

1. Leaders are motivated by one of two things: inspiration or desperation.

Inspiration. They're inspired by what network marketing is all about and what you offer with this business opportunity. Inspired by the number of people they can help. Inspired by the income. Inspired by having freedom in their lives.

Desperation. They're ready for change and they need something like this in their lives. Maybe they're living lives of quiet desperation. Maybe they're sick and tired of being sick and tired.

When I started my network marketing business, I was both inspired and desperate. If you can find that mix, you've identified a person motivated enough to become a leader.

2. The second significant identifier for me is that I'm excited to work with someone. We've all encountered distributors we dread even talking with on the phone. If you care about your business, your energy, and your wellbeing, I recommend you stop mentoring people

who have that effect on you. Don't work one-on-one with them.

A clear identifier that you have a leader worth working with is that you're excited to work with her. The energy, enthusiasm, and passion she has about the business fuels you. Working with someone like that, I get just as much out of the relationship as I give.

Sifting for Leaders

As I sift for potential leaders, I'm looking for these signs, in order of importance:

1. **They're winning challenges.** Leaders are competitive. Leaders want to be at the top. Leaders want to be winning. Somebody who wins the little challenges you run for your team may be a leader.

2. **They sign up distributors right away.** When someone on my team starts bringing in other people right away, that's a big identifier to me that I have a potential leader. This is a person I'm going to invest my one-on-one time in.

3. **They implement the trainings.** A leader wants more. Be careful, though – consuming information does not indicate a leader. If a person consumes information *and* signs people up, he is a potential leader you want to work with. But if he is just consuming information and not actually taking action, I won't spend one-on-one time with him.

4. **They are coachable**. Leaders are willing to take direction and follow your lead.

5. **They're helping others.** In a training or video chat, you'll notice people in the group who help others. They're in there answering questions. They always contribute. They find something of value and share it in the group.

Pay Attention to Sleeping Giants

When I refer to a "sleeping giant" I mean a person in your organization who hasn't taken any action yet, but who you know intuitively has the ability to build a strong business. You can see her potential. You can feel it when you talk to her. She's the type of person others are attracted to. People listen to her, people follow her, people look to her for what she has to say. Maybe she's not ready at this moment. Maybe she doesn't know she's a leader yet. Maybe she's not ready because of fear, because of self-doubt, because she's busy with other things. Maybe she doesn't see the big picture of network marketing yet. She doesn't see what's possible, but she's still a leader. She's just not ready to lead in this business.

When I have a potential leader in my organization who's not ready to lead in this business, I keep touching that sleeping giant. I was one, myself. I was a distributor for six months before I took action in this business. I signed up, and my sponsor, Bob, kept trying to get me to do something, but I wasn't yet inspired to action. I was a leader, just not in this realm yet. Eventually, six months after I signed up, I became inspired and took action. Then I went on to build a team of over 30,000 distributors. I was a sleeping giant in Bob's organization. He knew I had the ability to build a big business, so he kept touching the sleeping giant.

Hayley Christian

Hayley Christian, a distributor I personally sponsored, was also a sleeping giant. A distributor for three years, she had built her team to about 20 people working under her and was making a couple of hundred dollars a week. She hung out there, coasting. I kept reaching out to Hayley and connecting with her, though. All of the sudden, as a new year began, during five months – from January through May – she blew up her business. She made the decision to let go of the excuses and fears blocking her growth. And she totally took off! It's been an honor and an inspiration to work closely with Hayley and watch her grow. During that big push, she kept advancing, rank after rank. She started speaking on other team leaders' calls. She eventually spoke on our company's national call. She spoke at our leadership event. Hayley has since gone on to become a leader with a team of thousands of distributors. She was a sleeping giant. I intuitively knew she was able to succeed in this business, which is why I continued to work with her.

I encourage you to keep touching those sleeping giants. Let them know that you're ready when they're ready. A sleeping giant wants you to keep connecting with her. Don't depend on her. Go out there in search of other leaders. But do continue to believe in her. Continue to see what's possible for her. Continue to let her know you believe in her. "I believe in you" is probably the most important phrase you can offer to anyone – as long as it's truthful and you sincerely believe it. Follow it up with why you believe in that person and what you see as possible for her. That's how I love to touch sleeping giants. Keep connecting with them because they might come around.

Action Steps

1. Think back to the story I just shared about Hayley. Do you see yourself in Hayley *before* she made the shift? If so, make the decision now to change! It really is just a decision. If you have already made the shift and have a working downline, jump to Action Step #2.

2. If you already have a working downline and leaders in your organization, make two lists:
   a) Your leaders
   b) Your potential leaders

Chapter 9

WORKING THE NUMBERS

You don't lead by hitting people over the head —
that's assault, not leadership.
— Dwight D. Eisenhower

Five True Leaders

To attend the first corporate-sponsored training weekend of my network marketing career, I drove 12 hours from Boston to Washington, D.C., along with a few of my downline distributors and my personal sponsor, Bob. I was excited to get all the details of how to succeed in my new industry. The event began at 8 o'clock Saturday morning, and I was immediately mesmerized by the man leading the training. A concept he shared that morning has stuck with me for many years and helped mold the philosophy I now teach on building a network marketing business.

"You're really only looking for five people."

That statement simplified my outlook on my new business. Prior to hearing it, I thought I needed a team of hundreds, maybe even thousands of people to make this business happen. It was true that I needed big numbers, but I couldn't wrap my head around how I was going to recruit that many people. I couldn't wrap my head around how the duplication process could generate a big team. My mind couldn't even conceive, let alone believe, that I could build a team of, say, 5,000 distributors. But I *could* wrap my head around "you're only looking for five people." Those five people need to be five true leaders. Even so, finding five people – that I could get behind.

My take-away from that weekend was the simple concept that five true leaders was the number. When you get five true leaders in your downline, you have officially "made it." Eventually your five true leaders are going to develop their own five true leaders. That compounds to a team of 25 leaders. With 25 leaders in your downline, your business is no longer dependent on you. Your business will grow away from you, and it will continue to grow for years to come.

You are NOT looking for just five people though. Network marketing doesn't work that way. You are looking for five true leaders. You can find these five true leaders in a variety of ways, but the important piece is that your focus, your drive, your activities all point toward finding and developing five true leaders. This is different from signing up customers or distributors and hoping some would take off. Although I had to continue to do that, my focus was on finding my five true leaders. Prior to that corporate training weekend, I had noticed people in my company recruiting 20, 30, 40 people a month, which I used to strive for (and fall short). After that weekend, I no longer aimed to be a big recruiter. I aimed to bring in a few people a month, work closely with them, and sift through my downline to identify those five true leaders who were all in. The ones ready to build like I wanted to build. The ones who had a vision and a dream and would do whatever it took to succeed!

Leaders of Leaders Work Two Funnels

It takes a lot of action to connect to your five true leaders. You still have to work with all of your customers. You still have to work with all the distributors who sign up, talk a big game, and then do nothing. You still have to work with the people who come in and only do a little bit. And you still have to work with people who sign up, do a good amount, but never become a leader. They quit, fade away, or migrate to another company. You have to go through all that. You have to sift through large volumes of people to find leaders who are hungry to work with you.

I see our business as comprised of two "funnels" – one to find distributors and another to identify leaders within those distributors. The first funnel may look like this: you talk to 500 people about the business, 250 say they're going to look at it, 125 actually take a look, and 25 sign up as distributors. Most people understand that funnel, although they are usually surprised by the number of people they initially have to talk to.

The second funnel involves filtering through your distributors to find leaders. Here's a rough idea of how it looks. Twenty-five people come in as distributors intending to work the business. Of those 25, only 15 do anything. Of the 15 who do something, 5 actually become active, working distributors. They stick around. They're with you and your business for an extended period of time. One of those 5 will become a leader. That's how rare leaders are. It's not just one out of 25 that you're looking to sift through. We need to combine both funnels. We talked to 500 people to get one true leader. And I'm telling you that you need 5 leaders in total. *Wrap your mind around this.* It's a lot of work, but cultivating five true leaders gives you a business that means freedom in your life!

Fast or Slow, Find Your Five

During that same corporate weekend event in D.C., after the trainer laid out the five-leaders concept for us, he asked us how quickly we were going to find them. He talked about the energy, motivation, and determination required to find those five leaders. Then he told the following story.

Imagine you're sitting in the stands of a gymnasium, and down on the floor of the gymnasium are 10,000 little cups flipped upside down. Those 10,000 cups represent potential people you can talk with about this business. Under those 10,000 cups are five diamonds. Those diamonds represent five true leaders. How fast would you go down there? How fast would you start flipping the cups to find those five? If you flipped a few and didn't find a diamond, would you stop? Would you know which cups the diamonds were under?

Everyone wants to know how long it will take for this business to "take off" for them. "How many people do I have to talk to?" they ask. I don't know. It's rare, but maybe the first five cups you flip are the leaders you're looking for. Most likely not. Maybe you flip half the cups and you find all of your leaders. Maybe you flip all the cups except for five, and you don't find any leaders until those last five. I can't predict how long it's going to take you, but a sure way to fail is to stop "flipping cups."

Your skills, energy, momentum, passion, and the speed at which you connect with people about this business will determine when you find your five leaders. It's a numbers game, and you can increase the probability of finding leaders in two ways:

1. You can talk to more people, flipping more cups faster and faster, which requires sheer grit and hard work.

2. You can work on getting better. Better at presenting the business opportunity, better at talking to people, better at mastering your mindset, better at attracting team members.

Time Is the Great Equalizer

If you consider the leaders in your company or this industry as a whole, they may appear far ahead of you. It may seem like you can't get to where they are. It's true that you can't leapfrog your way to the top in a week or a month, but you *can* get there over time. Time is the great equalizer in our industry. Work your numbers, talk to as many people as you can, and continue to develop yourself as a human being and as a leader until you bring in five true leaders.

Action Step

Look at the lists of leaders and potential leaders you made in Chapter 8. Who are the distributors in your downline that you've been working with diligently yet they're not growing, they're just sucking energy out of you. Make the decision today to LET THEM GO. Stop trying to force something that isn't there. You're not doing yourself or them any favor by continuing to try to motivate them into action.

Chapter 10

THE BUILD-TO-LAST
MENTORSHIP SYSTEM

Leadership is unlocking people's potential to become better.
— Bill Bradley

Have an Upfront Understanding with People You Mentor

When you mentor people one-on-one, you must have an upfront understanding with them. During the recruiting and "getting started right" processes, you will already have laid the foundation for this understanding.

When someone first starts, you want them to know that you'll have an employee-employer relationship for the first few months. Distributors are not actually my employees, but their following my guidance sets them up to succeed. I also want people I mentor to know right away that I'm reliable. Many of us haven't had people we can depend on, so I want those I mentor to know I'm not going anywhere. I also want to know from them that they're not going anywhere and that their word is good. I make it clear right upfront that I'm going to match their efforts. They walk, I walk. They run, I run. They do nothing, I do nothing. That upfront mentor-mentee understanding needs to be in place before we start working together.

Be a Professional Mentor

As a "professional mentor," I'm available one-on-one, not just in groups. I'm available via text, phone call, direct message. I'm available if people want to meet face-to-face. In our weekly or monthly check-in call, it's me and the person I'm mentoring, one-on-one. I also randomly touch in on a daily basis with the leaders I'm developing. I send them texts and social media messages, and sometimes I'll just pick the phone up and call. That's the availability and commitment I make as a professional mentor.

For this to be workable for me and my family, I also establish clear boundaries from the start: when I'm working, I'm working, and when I'm off, I'm off. Today, as I write, I have five young kids at home. My business is set up so I don't work weekends and I don't work nights. At those times I'm with my family. I'm structured in this regard, and it's important for you too. Schedule your business hours and stick to them. That way you're able to be fully present and energized outside of work, and when you come to work, you're fully present and energized at work.

Mentorship Time with Your Leaders

I break down my business hours into three categories:
1. Recruiting
2. One-on-one mentoring of leaders
3. Group work with the team

In this section we'll focus on working with your

leaders. On specific days my sole focus is building leaders. When you're first starting out, this will be no more than one day a week. As your team grows, you could eventually devote two or three days a week to cultivating leaders.

When you're working with leaders, that's all you should be doing. You're not recruiting. You're not building your website. You're not working on social media. The hours I dedicate to mentoring my leaders fall into two categories: dedicated days for one-on-one mentoring calls and small chunks of time on non-mentoring days.

In addition to my dedicated hours, I spend time thinking about my leaders. For example, during my morning routine. On days I work with my leaders, I'm particular about getting my mind in the right space. I visualize my calls. I visualize how the day is going to go. I visualize my leaders not as they currently are, but as they can be. Even on non-mentoring days, I still spend time during my morning routine visualizing them at their highest possible level.

Structuring One-on-one Mentorship Calls

I connect with everyone I mentor on a weekly or monthly basis. We meet by phone, video conference, or face-to-face, for half an hour. I schedule weekly check-ins with leaders I'm running with. For those who have leadership potential but are not building aggressively at the moment, we do monthly check-ins. I also schedule monthly check-ins for those leaders who I have already mentored to the point they are running their own teams and don't need me as much anymore.

The structure for mentorship calls is as follows:

Catching up. The first five minutes we're connecting on a friendly, human level with a little chitchat. It's not serious, just catching up.

Transition. When it's time to transition from chitchat into actual mentorship, I say something positive about what they're doing and share my excitement to talk with them. It's an important part of the conversation because it prevents us from getting caught up in too much chitchat and clearly indicates it's time to focus on business.

Review key performance indicators (KPIs), highlighting the positive, addressing the negative. KPIs are specific, quantifiable, actionable benchmarks we can measure to determine whether or not leaders are on track to meet their goals. Ideally we set a mix of two personal and two team KPIs for a total of four. In the beginning, there might be three personal and only one team KPI because the leader's team is not yet that big.

Personal recruiting KPI examples:
- Number of new customer sign-ups in a week
- Number of new personally-sponsored distributors in a week
- Number of business presentations in a week
- Number of invites in a week

Team KPI examples:
- Number of new distributors coming into your downline in a week
- Number of rank advancements in your entire downline in a week
- Number of personally-sponsored distributors sponsoring another distributor in a week
- Number of personally-sponsored distributors rank-advancing in a week

During the previous week, we would have set KPIs for this week. When we're on the call together, I want to know if the leader I'm mentoring hit her KPIs or not, what worked, and what didn't work during the week. At this point in the conversation, I address any negatives and accentuate any positives.

Set KPIs for the upcoming week. In the beginning I set KPIs for those I mentor, but eventually they set their own KPIs.

A good ending. I want leaders I mentor to leave the call feeling excited to go out there and take action, and I want them to know I believe in their ability to succeed at the highest levels. I end my one-on-one calls saying, "Tell me again about your vision. What's your ultimate dream for you and your family?" I want them to repeat that to me each time we talk.

BONUS 8-minute audio and accompanying PDF detailing this call available at *www.KeithCallahan.com/book.*

One-on-one Daily Check-Ins

On days that are not dedicated to working with my leaders, I want to connect quickly. I'll usually spend 15 minutes and send out supportive, inspirational messages to people I'm mentoring.

These connections are less formal than our dedicated weekly call. These text messages, phone calls, Facebook messages, a quick card or note, and the like, are meant to keep the energy, excitement, and personal relationship going. I continuously let my leaders know I believe in them, I'm here for them, I'm running with them, and I'm not going anywhere.

Group Mentorship

In addition to one-on-one mentorship, I also work with my leaders in a group. There are two main ways I do that:

- A weekly video conference for my leaders to come together, inspire each other, and share leadership principles.

- An online social-media forum (currently a Face-book group) where we're in communication throughout the day, again, inspiring each other and sharing leadership principles.

Action Steps

1. Make a list of those in your downline that you want to mentor one-on-one, and print a copy of my mentorship calls template for each person. Mentorship calls template available at *www.KeithCallahan.com/book*.

2. Set up one-on-one mentorship calls with the leaders and potential leaders on your list.

3. Conduct your first mentorship call with each leader, setting KPIs for the upcoming week.

Chapter 11

BUILDING TRUST

True leadership stems from individuality that is
honestly and sometimes imperfectly expressed...
Leaders should strive for authenticity over perfection.
— Sheryl Sandberg

In order to develop the leaders around us, we must gain their trust. Following is the process I've developed, refined, and use to gain the trust of leaders I mentor.

Our Job Is Developing Human Beings

As leaders of leaders, our real job is developing human beings. Uncovering human potential. Bringing out the best in people. Meeting them where they are and seeing where they can go. Helping them see themselves not as they are but as they can be.

In an earlier chapter, I made the distinction between "a leader of leaders" and "a leader of followers." A leader of followers doesn't do the work of truly developing other human beings, whereas it's the core of what leaders of leaders do. We go deep with those we mentor to develop their potential, shift how they look at the world and solve problems. We work with their thoughts, their habits, their daily practices. We work to increase their self-esteem. We recognize their dormant potential, and our job is facilitating the emergence of that potential.

Not everyone is willing to do the work of realizing their potential. For reasons we've explored, not everyone will become a leader on your team. Leaders are rare. Leaders want to grow at a deep, core level. They want to change. In order for you to guide someone through this growth process, building trust is imperative.

Trust Is the Foundation of Successful Mentorship

When you're mentoring people who want to run with this business, you'll know. They're doing all the work, all the daily activities, reaching out, following up, presenting the business. They're ready to build to the next level. In order to get there, they have to grow as a person. For me to help them grow, I need to be able to speak truth into their lives and have them receive it. This is where trust comes into play. Until they trust me, they won't be willing to share their REAL internal blocks or receive my guidance.

Six months ago, a distributor in my downline (not personally sponsored) connected with me. Let's call her Nina. For two years Nina had consistently brought in new distributors and customers. She was earning $250 to $500 a week, but she didn't have any working distributors on her team. She was ready to take her business to the next level.

Nina and I started one-on-one calls. She was eager and constantly reaching out to me, but not yet willing to open up about what was going on inside. The work we do as leaders is not all that different from being a life coach or therapist, from my perspective. When I start working one-on-one with new people, they're usually focused on question like: "How do I start doing this?" or "How do I talk to this person?" or "What would I say in this situation?" or "How do I get better at advertising on social media platforms?" They want to know how to do the *activities* better. What I want to get to, though, is real personal growth. To do that level of work together, we must establish trust. I needed Nina to trust me so I could speak truth into her life. Without that trust, I can't mentor people to help them develop into the leaders they're capable of being.

Eventually there was a bond of trust between Nina and me. Once we started talking about what was really going on – her fears, her limiting beliefs, her self-esteem, the lacks and limitations she placed upon herself – everything opened up for her and her business flourished.

How do you know when you've built trust with a person? Most often, it's during the conversation when she feels safe enough to expresses true emotion – anger, sadness, fear, desperation, hopelessness. Maybe she's ready to quit. Maybe she thinks it's too hard. Eventually she surrenders. There's a surrender of the mind to the heart. A surrender of the ego self to the higher self. That might sound "foo foo," but it truly is a surrender of control. It comes about with crying, frustration, giving up, and then – once someone fully surrenders and says, "I'm willing to do whatever it takes" – that's when we have the trust. That is when our work together really starts.

Modeling Behavior

Your leadership position isn't one of title or authority. It's a mentoring-by-modeling position. You have to do what you say you're going to do. You have to do what you're asking others to do. You have to walk your own walk, go through your own stuff, grow into and express your own personal human potential.

Be all in. You have to be 100 percent in, no questions asked, no back door, no escape route, no way out. All in on your business. All in on yourself. All in on the person you're mentoring. All in on the company you're with. All in on our industry. You cannot fake being all in. If, in the back of your mind, doubts creep in (and you entertain them), you will lose your credibility and your influence over the people you mentor. They can feel it. They'll know it. If you look at the best leaders – in business, in sports, in the military, in politics – they're all in on the mission, on the cause. That's what you must model.

Be vulnerable. You also want to be vulnerable. You don't have to be perfect. Nobody can relate to that. Talk about your fears. Talk about your insecurities. When you're mentoring people, tell stories about how you went through similar experiences to theirs. Your vulnerability increases how much they're willing to share with you. As you share limitations and areas you're working on, those you mentor will feel safer sharing worries, limitations, and areas they're working on.

Paint the Vision

Painting the vision is about getting people to see themselves not as they are but as they can be. Letting them know what's possible for them in this business. Letting them know how big an opportunity this is. Getting the "leaving a legacy" vision in their minds.

Paint that vision over and over. Paint the vision that they're capable. Paint the vision that they can do it. Together, paint the vision of what their life is going to be like…when they make that first X amount of dollars.

When that credit card is paid off. When they get to say goodbye to their boss. When that extra thousand dollars is coming in each month.

Paint a vision both short-term and long-term — after they've passed on. You're helping them to dream a big, beautiful, bold dream of what life can be like. I help people paint *their* vision of doing what they want, when they want, with who they want.

Your belief holds the space for *their* vision until *they* believe it. At least once every time I talk to one of my leaders, I let him know I believe in him. When I end a mentoring call saying, "Tell me your dream again," I visualize it as he tells me. I can see his dream and feel it in my own heart. I know it's possible for him.

My Mentor Helped Me Paint the Vision

On an early phone call with my mentor, Craig, he asked where I saw myself going with this business. I shared that I wanted to make $1 million a year.

Craig: How is it going to feel, Keith, when you make your first million?

Me: A dream fulfilled! I'll be able to tithe and support causes my wife and I care about. I'll be able to provide for my family without any worries.

Craig: I can't wait to celebrate it with you. I believe it, brother. I know you can do it.

Those words came from his heart. Craig truly believed in me and my ability to do it. Imagine the power of that for me. The power of a mentor I respect really believing in me. Without his belief I wouldn't have had the courage to go after my dreams.

Never underestimate the power of simply believing in the person you're mentoring. We all need someone who believes in us.

Consistency

Trust is built over time. It's not a matter of a couple of phone calls. When someone needs you and you are there, trust is built. When you show up to every call. When you're present – emotionally, mentally, physically, spiritually – trust is built. When you say you're going to do something and you do it, trust is built.

Day after day, week after week, month after month, year after year, you're there showing up. You're not perfect, but you're there. You make mistakes, but you're there. You get frustrated with them and they get frustrated with you, but you both continue to show up. That builds trust over time.

Be a Mentor First and a Friend Second

One of the biggest mistakes I see would-be leaders in our industry make is emphasizing friendship over mentorship. Don't get me wrong, I am dear friends with almost everybody I mentor. We've gone to each other's weddings, laughed with each other, cried with each other, vacationed together. We've visited each other's newborn children in the hospital, like close friends do. But when we initially began working together, I was their mentor first. As a professional mentor, my goal is not to become their friend. That is secondary. My goal is to mentor them to achieve their goals.

Say What They Need to Hear, Not What They Want to Hear

During another early call with Craig, I shared how excited I was about this business and couldn't wait to start working with him. I shared my million-dollar-a-year vision and all the things I wanted to accomplish. I went on and on, talking about my goals, my dreams, my desires, my work ethic, and how much I was willing to do. Craig listened to me ramble on for half an hour, and then he said, "You know what? We're in the business of helping people. You just told me all the different things you want to accomplish, all the goals that you want to achieve, and I didn't once hear you talking about how much you care for other people and how much you want to help other people. To be honest, I don't even know if you do, because I never heard it."

It was a huge punch in the gut. We ended the call, I went downstairs, and my wife, Amy, asked me how the conversation went. I told her, and she said, "Wow. You were so excited about this call, and you're so deflated now."

I *was* deflated, but I had to hear those words from Craig. I had to learn to be in service. If I had had a mentor who didn't want to offend me and just said, "Yeah, Keith, go get those goals. You're going to be great!" instead of saying, "You know what, Keith, those things are all awesome, but you didn't share once about how you want to help other people, and that's what our industry is all about," then I would never have grown into the role of being in service.

Lovingly speak truth to the people you mentor. Don't be afraid they're going to leave. If they leave, they weren't the right ones. If they *are* the right ones, when you speak truth into their lives, they will receive what you offer and grow. They might not initially like it. They might get aggravated. They might not be accustomed to people talking to them with such forthrightness, but if you speak from the heart, if you speak in a nurturing way that pushes them to become more than who they are, they will trust and respect you.

Action Steps

This is not a one-time action. You must make the following four decisions and commit to growing into each of them. Remind yourself of these disciplines until they become part of who you are:

1. Make the decision to be "all in" on your business.
2. Make the decision to be vulnerable with your leaders.
3. Make the decision to be consistent with your leaders.
4. Make the decision to be honest with your leaders.

Chapter 12

HELPING MENTEES CROSS BRIDGES

Leaders must be close enough to relate to others,
but far enough ahead to motivate them.
— John Maxwell

About a year into my network marketing business, I decided I wanted an office outside of our house. I rented an attic studio in a rundown building. On the only flat wall, I hung a picture of a footbridge over a river. I spent a lot of time meditating on that bridge picture. It was symbolic of the importance of being a "bridge" for the distributors I mentored. The bridge represented the full arc of bringing in a new distributor through developing her into a leader of leaders. The large bridge comprises many small bridges.

Case Study: Liz Hartke Crossing All Bridges

I'd like to share an abridged (ha!) story about Liz Hartke.

The Bridge of Becoming a Customer

The company I work with distributes health and wellness products, as I've mentioned. When Liz saw my flyer in a yoga studio, she called me. Eventually she became a customer. She started using the product and crossed the first bridge – trying new products. She used our products for a couple of months and started seeing good results. During these months as a customer getting results, Liz became an advocate for the product. She was also watching me on Facebook. She saw what I posted and eventually reached out again. This time she wanted to hear about the business opportunity.

The Bridge of Becoming a Distributor

Quick side note. Liz reached out on a Friday. I'm a husband and father whose main priority is my family. I messaged Liz back saying something to the effect of, "I'd love to talk with you, but I don't work on weekends as I reserve that time for my family." I got back to Liz first thing Monday morning. One of the reasons she was excited to talk with me, she told me, is that I had boundaries in my life. People are watching everything you do; make sure you're modeling professional and balanced behavior.

Liz had already crossed the first bridge – going from being unsure to enthusiastic about a product. Now she was considering crossing the second bridge. She believed in the products but wasn't sure about the business opportunity. During our first few calls, my belief in and enthusiasm for this business opportunity were passed on to Liz, which helped her sign up as a distributor. She crossed that second bridge.

The Bridge of Becoming a Working Distributor

As a distributor, Liz began talking to her friends and family right away. And just like everyone who starts in network marketing, Liz encountered stumbling blocks. She struggled right from the beginning – with people who questioned what she was doing, with the challenge of reaching out to talk to people. Little by little, though, Liz persevered. Within two months of working the business, she hit her initial goal of Diamond: the first, major, recognized rank in our company. When Liz hit that rank, we celebrated her. She had crossed the bridge of becoming a working distributor.

The Bridge of Entering Leadership

With her early success, Liz's excitement about this business grew. She wanted to start bringing in working distributors, not just discount distributors. Once Liz made that decision, our relationship changed. I saw her more as a partner. I started spending more time with her. She started attracting people who were interested in the business opportunity, and I often got on the phone with them to help Liz present the business. We started connecting multiple times a day via text messaging, social media, video conferencing, and phone calls. We met up once a week. Liz was aggressively building her business now. Eventually, she found her first true leader. She had crossed the next bridge.

The Bridge of Becoming a Leader of Leaders

Our company has local, quarterly, in-person events. Liz was terrified of public speaking, nonetheless she messaged me one day saying, "I want to speak at the next event." At that time 200 to 300 people attended the events. I arranged for her to make a presentation. I remember sitting in the audience with her husband, Michael. When Liz got up to speak at the event, I could see she was that palms-sweaty, voice-shaky, about-to-throw-up kind of nervous. Her first presentation was – let's just say – not stellar, but she did it. Then Liz started speaking a bit more and a bit more.

Fast forward to the present. Liz now speaks at the larger corporate events, addressing 20,000-plus people. She's hit the top ranks in our company and her distributors have started to hit those top ranks. Liz is now a leader of leaders and doesn't need me anymore. You've done it right when those you mentor don't need you anymore. They can do everything you've taught them – even better than you can. That's the goal.

The ultimate goal of a leader who is building to last, is to walk people across their many small bridges as far as they are willing to go. Some will cross one or two bridges, some a few more, and a handful will go all the way with you.

Case Study, Hayley Christian: Crossing Leadership Bridges

A real leader will not stick around in this industry if she's bored; she needs to be learning and growing. She needs something to strive for. When I have a real leader, I start pushing her and challenging her. I also start exposing her to my larger team. Exposing an emerging leader to the rest of my team serves the individual and it also helps the people on my team because a new, enthusiastic leader brings vibrancy. She brings fresh ways of doing business. She's green, she's excited. I like to expose my team to that energy. It also challenges the emerging leader.

Let's look at a recent situation, when Hayley Christian was emerging as a leader.

I and four other leaders – not within my downline but within the parent company – were running a five-week leadership training. Each of us was responsible for one week of the training. In order to help Hayley move deeper into her leadership role, we did two things during this training:

1. I brought Hayley into all of my conversations with the other four leaders. This made them aware of Hayley's skills and talent, and built her self-esteem because she recognized herself as these leaders' peer.

2. I was responsible for kicking off the first week of the training, which meant doing a live video training in a private Facebook group – Monday through Friday. I gave Hayley one of those days, which meant the opportunity to address a large audience. This put her way out

of her comfort zone, and she stepped up. She did it.

A few weeks later, we flew a bunch of distributors on the team to the Boston area for a weekend retreat. I asked Hayley to fly in and do a presentation. She was scared to death, but she gave a strong presentation. All of the sudden, leaders from other teams within our company were reaching out to Hayley to have her speak on their calls.

Then Hayley got invited to speak at one of our national corporate conventions. Then she got to speak on our national call. Then she got to speak at a leadership event. Most of those opportunities, Hayley got on her own. They were no longer doors I opened. But it all started with my putting Hayley out of her comfort zone and challenging her.

Open doors for your leaders, prop them up. Don't make the mistake of doing it yourself because you can currently do it better. Your end game is developing other leaders. Give them that opportunity. Start small – have them be a guest speaker on a team call – and then move them up.

Prepare the Leader

One of your responsibilities is preparing an emerging leader for the income, responsibility, and recognition coming in. I don't know if you've heard the statistics, but something like 80 or 90 percent of people who win the lottery end up bankrupt. Why? Because they have a windfall of money that they're not prepared for. It's not that they're reckless or dumb. It's that they do reckless and dumb things because they're not ready for the energy that comes with all that money. You've heard stories about the professional athletes and actors and performers who've lost all their money. It's because no one helped prepared them for enormous success.

We need to prepare our leaders on how to handle

the income that's coming in, on how to handle the responsibility that's coming their way, on how to handle all of the recognition. It's the final bridge to cross.

Action Steps

Succeeding in our industry requires crossing a series of bridges. Knowing where you're at and the next bridge to cross gives you a clear next step in your business growth.

1. Think about yourself and your business. What is the next bridge you need to cross? What key skills do you need to acquire and actions do you need to take to cross that bridge?

2. Think about each of your leaders and potential leaders. What is the next bridge each one of them needs to cross? What are the key skills they need to acquire and actions they need to take?

Chapter 13

LET THEM LEAVE THE NEST

People ask the difference between a leader and a boss.
The leader leads, and the boss drives.
— Theodore Roosevelt

Once you've got your leaders all the way to the other side of the final bridge and prepared them to handle what's there, you have one final thing to do for those you mentor: get out of their way.

Case Study, Tony (The Icon) Furtado: Sometimes You Have to Get out of the Way from the Start

When I became a distributor, one of the first people I signed up was Nicole Jones (who I mentioned earlier). Nicole and I went to high school together, and we reconnected through Facebook. She saw me sharing our products, reached out to me, and became a discount distributor.

Within the first couple months of Nicole's business,

she signed up Tony Furtado. Tony was one of those distributors you dream about. He ran with this business right away. If you look at the timeline, it's me signing up, then right away I sign up Nicole (who has had enormous success), then Nicole signs up Tony, and he goes on to have enormous success. Tony was a born leader. Nicole and I had to just get out of his way.

The biggest mistake we can make with leaders who are fully ready to run with this business on their own is holding them back, trying to tell them, "You should do it this way. You should do it that way." Right from the start Tony was flourishing with his own team, doing business his way. Maybe once a week, I would have a call with him, and then it turned into once a month. I was working with Craig at that time and on calls with Tony, I simply shared what Craig had shared with me.

Tony went on to build a business built to last. He's made millions of dollars. He's helped hundreds of thousands of people. And he's done it all on his own, his unique way. He's done it without much mentoring. He's one of those self-taught types. When you have someone like that, you just have to get out of the way and let him do his thing!

Control Versus Courage

As your team starts to grow, don't make the mistake many leaders in this industry make. They create an environment that emphasizes "their" team. That is good for followers, but it's a turn-off to potential leaders. It has enormous negative impact on the growth of a team. I've witnessed this a few times with leaders who wanted to control everything. They didn't want anybody else starting a "sub-team." They saw distributors only as a part of their team. They didn't see people in their downline as growing their own teams. Everyone had to focus on *their* team name. It was *their* team page. *Their* way was the way everyone should do things. They wanted to be the only leader.

Instead of focusing on being the one leader of the "whole" team, be a leader of leaders who has a team of teams. This business is about duplication of leadership. That's how you build to last. And it takes courage. It takes knowing your worth. It takes the ability to trust others. It takes being a person who doesn't need the spotlight. Ultimately, it takes having enough self-esteem to allow those you mentor to do this business better than you.

Knowing When the Leader Is Ready

I had a ton of fun working with Liz Hartke. We worked closely as partners building this business together. When we first got started, I mentored Liz, doing everything we've talked about in this book. I'd taken her through all of the stages. In our final stages, we were doing a lot together – team calls, team trainings, helping each other with prospects.

Eventually Liz started to grow away from me and not need me anymore on multiple levels. She started to need her own space to create in her way, to thrive and prosper. This is the most exciting time in your business if you are emotionally ready for it. It's like having a child going off to college. You nurtured this child, raised this child, got her to a certain point, and then as the child gets older, into high school and beyond, you start becoming friends with the child. You're no longer the teacher for the child, but someone who's inspired by and learning from the child. You become equals.

At some point the child goes off to college and needs to fly. She needs to experiment, to live her own life, to become parent of her own children, and all that. In network marketing, when you're working with a real leader, you have to give her the room to fly. If you push the leader correctly from the start – encouraging her, giving her opportunities – you'll know when it's time. You'll know when she's ready. If you're aware enough, you'll recognize that there's a certain point at which you're stifling rather than catalyzing the leader's growth.

When you have a true leader, you'll know she's ready when she starts moving away from you. The biggest blessing you can offer is to let her go. The biggest impediment to her growth and your growth, is to try to control that situation and keep that leader close to you. Let her fly.

What to Do When They Leave the Nest

Get out of the way and let them go. It's not any more complicated than that. Let them do their own thing. Don't try to coach them anymore. Again, it's like a child going off to college. When the child is at college, you lose the right to constantly check in, to see what time they're getting home, to know what they're doing, to know where they are. You have to give that child space. Just like a parent, when they're ready to leave the nest, let go. Give them the space they need.

Be available when they need you. Once they've gone, be like that parent who has a child at college. Metaphorically speaking, they're going to come back for summers. They're going to need you again. They're going to call you when things aren't working well. As a parent of five children, I can tell you all your children are different. So the amount of "need" from each is different. Some children are going to go away and never come back. Some children go away, and they need their parents a little bit. Some children go away, and they call their parents every day. When we're working with leaders, it's the same. Think about it like a parent and be available when they need you.

Continue to partner with them. I love to continue

working with leaders when they leave the nest. I continue to partner with them on trainings, on retreats, on big calls that we put together. If we're going to do a 30-day or a 60-day competition, I'll see if that leader wants to do it with me.

Enjoy their friendship. Most of my friends are in this industry because we think alike, we act alike, we see the world the same way, and we love talking about business, creating, and entrepreneurship. I'm now good friends with all the leaders I once mentored.

Action Steps

1. Think about the leaders in your organization. Are there any you're holding back? Any you need to push out of the nest? If so, make a plan to do so this week.

2. Think about the leaders who have already gone off on their own. Reach out to them. Let them know you're there if they need anything and you appreciate them.

3. Think about the leaders in your organization. Who can you partner with for the next promotion, event, or training?

4. Enjoy the time with your leaders!

AFTERWORD

Now you know where to start and what to do to become a leader of leaders. Will you succeed? You're answer to the following question is the one true predictor:

How much do you want to become a leader of leaders in our industry?

This sounds over-simplified, but it's not. More than 90 percent of the people who read this book will not move past their current level of success in network marketing. How bad you want it is the ultimate determinant. In explaining this to potential leaders, I always share the following excerpt about Hell Week from navyseals.com.

Hell Week consists of 5½ days of cold, wet, brutally difficult operational training on fewer than 4 hours of sleep. Hell Week tests physical endurance, mental toughness, pain and cold tolerance, teamwork, attitude, and your ability to perform work under high physical and mental stress, and sleep deprivation. Above all, it tests determination and desire. On average, only 25% of SEAL candidates make it through Hell Week, the toughest training in the U.S. Military. It is often the greatest achievement of their lives, and with it comes the realization that they can do

20X more than they ever thought possible. It is a defining moment that they reach back to when in combat. They know that they will never, ever quit or let a teammate down.

Over the years, research has been done to determine a common trait in those individuals who make it through Hell Week, without definitive answer. They are not necessarily the largest or strongest men, nor the fastest swimmers, but those with burning desire to be SEALs. Instructors have observed only one true predictor of which candidates will ultimately succeed – it's those who want it the most – you can see it in their EYES!

To achieve success at the highest levels in your business, you are not going to endure anything near what a Navy SEAL candidate does – on a physical level. But becoming a leader of leaders in this industry requires the same determination and desire of the SEALs who make it through Hell Week. Our industry will test you. How badly do you want it? How determined are you? Just like the Navy SEAL instructors have observed one true predictor in their SEAL candidates, you can predict your own success.

Can You See It in Your Own Eyes?

Wherever you are, whatever you're doing at this very moment, stop and pause. Make the decision to want this more than anything else in your life. Your success depends on it.

Next steps.

I suggest you read this book from beginning to end once every quarter for the next two years. That is a lot, I know. It's important to do so. Each re-reading will reinforce pieces of the *Build to Last* process that you're implementing. You will also recognize pieces you did not see the last time you read the book. The more you study this book and remind yourself of our way of building, the more natural it will become for you.

If you haven't done so yet, also be sure to go to *www.keithcallahan.com/book* and download all the FREE bonuses mentioned in *Build to Last*. In addition, you can opt to be notified when any new books, products, or programs come out.

Now go out there and become the next network marketing leader. I believe in you and know you have what it takes.

Much love,
Keith

A CALL TO ACTION
FROM LIZ HARTKE

Probably similar to you, Keith Callahan came into my life when I least expected it, but most needed it. I was at a crossroads in my life. I was either going to rise to the calling that was put on my heart or accept life as it was for the next several decades. Like many people do, I went to college, got a "good job," and nestled into my cubicle and the monotonous routine that comes with mediocrity and acceptance.

But to my core, I was unsettled. I knew I was made for something more, but I felt paralyzed as to how I could bring that truth into the light.

At the same time that I was grossly unfulfilled in my job, I was more than 50 pounds overweight, trying to nurture relationships that didn't serve me, and disconnected from the value systems I claimed to hold dear. I was living someone else's idea of what my life should look like, and I was at a breaking point.

I remember sitting in my climate-controlled cube scribbling down business ideas that would someday be my big break! The entrepreneurial spirit was always within me, but I was living as a dreamer at the time, never really taking action. I guess I thought that somehow "time" was going to get me to where I ultimately wanted to go, when in reality, time is a thief. Every passing moment that I wasn't working toward my daydream took me further from it.

After writing up one of many formal business plans that I was very excited about, I brought it to a friend who is a lawyer in the business realm. Within 10 minutes he had torn it to shreds and written me a list of all I would need to do to even get one foot out the door on this brilliant mess of mine.

I realized that I either had to do the legwork on this thing to make it happen or I had to seriously consider figuring out how to like my life the way it was.

And just at the right time – as I was about to trade in my dream for freedom and fulfillment for a life sentence in my cubicle – I was introduced to my ticket to freedom. I didn't know it at the time (as a matter of fact, ask Keith, I actually said NO to it four or five times before I opened my mind to network marketing), but I was being given the gift that I had so desperately wanted all along: a platform to live out my passions and purpose that would reward me in ways I never knew possible (financially and otherwise) without the stress of overhead and infrastructure.

Originally, I had reached out to Keith to conquer my health struggles. It was time to go all in on finding a healthy long-term approach to weight loss. I had no idea that there was a potential business opportunity connected to the products and systems he sold. I innocently picked up a brochure in some yoga studio, and there was Keith's name and email on the back.

I dove in on my health and saw my body transform. That was just the confidence I needed to see what I was capable of. The fire inside me to do more with my life was burning like never before!

But I still didn't have a plan…

Until one day I was scrolling Facebook on a random weekday and saw this guy out on a mid-day hike with his beautiful wife and kids. It was Keith, the nice bald dude I had bought the shakes from.

"What does this guy do that he can be out hiking in the middle of the day?" I wondered. I flashed to all of those values I said I held dear but wasn't living by:

Family connection

Freedom of time

Adventure

Health

That morning, a gorgeous summer day, the sun was shining, and there I was stuck in traffic on my hour-long commute to my version of hell when the emotions I had successfully squashed for the last few years came flooding into me. Seeing that picture of Keith and his family, it finally hit me – "There's another way to live, and I'm not living it."

I pulled my car over into a parking lot. My hands were shaking, and I had tears streaming down my face. I felt like fear and anger and excitement were all boiling over at the same time. I grabbed my phone and I messaged Keith. "Fine. I'll learn more about what it is you do, but don't try to twist my arm. It just can't hurt to hear about it and then I'll decide…"

I still look back once in a while and thank God I sent that message.

That day I was introduced to what network marketing really is and what it's really not. All of my misconceptions were just that – wrong ideas. I didn't know I could build network marketing as a side hustle until it replaced my corporate income (and eventually multiplied it by more than 20 times).

But Keith's initial nudge to this business platform is the least of what he has done for my family and me. As months passed and I decided to go all in on this opportunity, there were times I would connect with Keith and ask questions regarding how to grow my business. I was fishing for a "Liz, do A, B, C, and you'll get D" kind of response only to find Keith on the other end of the phone pushing me beyond where I had ever been pushed before.

Almost never were his answers technical. He made me become resourceful and taught me that those kind of answers could be found on my own time if I wanted to know them badly enough (resources are boundless and a successful network marketer quickly learns that "I don't know" is a BS excuse). But Keith had this knack for challenging me to dig deeper and focus more on the person and leader I was born to become.

He knew that achieving a number or a rank would be a fleeting joy, but fulfilling my purpose through this platform would help me grow into leadership that would take me to the next level not only in my business, but in my marriage, motherhood, friendship, and entrepreneurship. He is the first person in my life who believed fully in me and then showed me the way.

Keith knows I'm not a very touchy-feely type – actually, we joke about it a lot – but I'm willing to put this into writing for the world to see because it couldn't be more true: Keith Callahan has been one of the greatest sources of light, truth, and leadership in my life, and I'm humbled by his belief in me and how he has loved me through this amazing journey! I think that's the secret – love. He has always had my best interest as a whole person at heart.

He may have introduced me to the business opportunity that transformed my family's life (I write this from our dream farmhouse in the country, both my husband and I retired from the rat race before the age of 30 to pursue our passions), but he introduced me to the person that God has called me to become and led me there by example.

Success in this business (in any business, really, but especially network marketing) rises and falls on leadership.

The best advice I could give to someone who comes out of reading this book with some fire inside to go for their dreams is to stoke that fire starting today! You, too, will be presented with opportunities and challenges along the way, and it's up to you to rise to them.

Leadership is a choice. It's cultivated through action, growth, vision, and how quickly (if at all) you get back up after each and every failure along the way.

Sure, I had Keith, but now so do you. The wisdom in these pages are the words he shared with me over and over since I started my journey.

If you are at your fork in the road, remember that the choice from here is yours and yours only. Thankfully, I got to a place where my fear of failure finally got trumped by my fear of life remaining the same, and I saw how this business platform was the vehicle to my new life.

What you choose today determines your tomorrow. Choose wisely and act swiftly. Life is too short to do otherwise.

Elizabeth "Liz" Hartke

ACKNOWLEDGEMENTS

Writing a book with the hope of selling thousands, maybe even millions of copies is not a solo project. *Build to Last* could not have come to fruition without the entire team.

First, I'd like to thank my wife, Amy, who walks this planet with such grace. You believed in me and supported me every step of the way. I truly am "the luckiest."

Thank you to my children, Dakota, Daphne, Wyatt, Adeline, and Emmett, for allowing Papa time in his office doing the work I am put on this earth to do. I love each of you with all my heart.

Thank you to my dad. The fortitude I learned from modeling you brought this book to the finish line. Thank you to my mom for your unconditional love and support all the years of my life.

Thank you to Craig Holiday for teaching us the heart and soul of network marketing. B2B.

Thank you to my editor, Jane Bernstein. Your love of the written word and dedication to this project weave through every page. I could not have done this without you.

Lastly, I am deeply grateful to every single distributor on my team, with a special acknowledgement to the leaders who have built their own teams. You know who you are. Continue to dream big and dream beautiful.

ABOUT THE AUTHOR

Keith Callahan is a husband, father, mentor, entre-
preneur and philanthropist. Since becoming financially
free at the age of 36, he spends his time helping others
identify, begin to create, and eventually realize the life
they were meant to live. *www.KeithCallahan.com*